Help for hurting Christians

Help for hurting Christians

Reflections on Psalms

Derek Thomas

 EVANGELICAL PRESS

EVANGELICAL PRESS
12 Wooler Street, Darlington, Co. Durham, DL1 1RQ, England
© Evangelical Press 1991

First published 1991

British Library Cataloguing in Publication Data available

ISBN 0 85234 284 5

Printed in Great Britain by the Bath Press, Avon

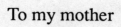

To my mother

Contents

Introduction

When, in the course of his turbulent love for Lydia Grenfell, the missionary to Persia, Henry Martyn, tried to sort out his conflicting emotions (whether to marry Lydia or forsake her for Asia and the call of God) he chose to learn Psalm 119 by heart. On the fateful morning when the urgent call came to him to join H.M.S. *Union,* he was in the middle of reading this great psalm to Lydia. Martyn's eventual usefulness for God as a missionary, choosing obedience to him before the emotional sway of his own heart, no doubt stems from his knowledge of this psalm.[1]

The psalms are meant to help us in difficult times

They are God's answer to Christians in trouble. This is because the book of Psalms is written (from a human point of view) by men in covenant with God. The gods of the nations could not be trusted. They were irrational and capricious. But Israel's God was different. His ways were reliable. His dealings with his people were predictable. God had laid down in writing how he would come to the aid of his people when they called upon him with sincere hearts. That is why one of the psalms we shall be looking at can say with such confidence:

> 'But let all those rejoice who put their trust in you;
> Let them ever shout for joy, because you defend them;
> Let those also who love your name be joyful in you'
>
> (Ps. 5:11).

God has promised to behave in a certain way. And he will not let us down.

Finding God's help in times of need through the psalms is what

Christians have been doing all through the centuries. That is why the book of Psalms has been held in such high esteem. Athanasius referred to it as 'an epitome of the whole Scriptures'; Basil called it 'a compendium of all theology'; Luther described it as 'a little Bible, and a summary of the Old Testament'; Melancthon called it 'the most elegant work extant in the world'; and Calvin said it was 'an anatomy of all the parts of the soul', and this because 'There is not an emotion of which anyone can be conscious that is not here represented as in a mirror.'[2]

According to Calvin, what we have in the psalms is a believer examining himself in God's presence, beckoning us to do the same. As we read them, it is as though we see ourselves in a mirror. No human emotion is concealed. They teach us what we should say when we come to God in prayer: 'Whatever may serve to encourage us when we are about to pray to God, is taught us in this book ... [it] makes known to us the privilege, which is desirable above all others, that not only is there opened up to us familiar access to God, but also that we have permission and freedom granted us to lay open before him our infirmities, which we would be ashamed to confess before men.'[3]

The psalms are full of Christ

Another feature emerges from the fact that the psalms are the poetry of God's covenant relationship with us: they are full of Jesus Christ! There seems little doubt that Jesus was fond of the psalms. On the cross he quotes three of them from memory: 'My God, my God, why have you forsaken me?' (Ps. 22:1); 'I thirst' (a reference to Ps. 69:21); and 'Into your hand I commit my spirit' (Ps. 31:5).

Now, it might be possible to argue that these words were given supernaturally to Christ on the cross. More probable, however, is the view that he learnt them as a young boy in Nazareth and often repeated and reflected upon them during his days of ministry. The psalms were the source of Jesus' strength and consolation, the powerful impulses in his life to fulfil his Father's will. In them he saw himself portrayed.

Living in the psalms will help us walk in his footsteps: 'Righteousness will go before him, and shall make his footsteps our pathway' (Ps. 85:13); 'For to this you were called, because Christ also suffered for us, leaving us an example, that you should follow his steps' (1 Peter 2:21).

It is an astonishing fact, not always appreciated, that the book of Psalms is quoted more often than any other book in the New Testament. As we have seen, Jesus was fond of the Psalms. So, too, was Paul. Of all the quotations the apostle uses from the Old Testament, one-fifth are from the psalms.[4] He uses the psalms to underline the universality of sin (Rom. 3:10-18; cf. Ps. 5; 10; 36); the blessedness of justification by faith (Rom. 4:6-8; cf. Ps. 32), the rejection of the gospel by Israel (Rom. 11:9-10; cf. Ps. 69); and the sufferings of Christ and all believers who follow him (Rom. 15:1-4; cf. Ps. 69). When Paul and his companions were asked to deliver the closing address at a meeting in Pisidian Antioch, they chose a message about Jesus Christ, alluding to two of the psalms (Ps. 2; 16).

The book of Hebrews also has a special place for the psalms. Out of thirty-six quotations from the Old Testament in the book of Hebrews, fifteen are from the psalms.[5]

The immediate appeal of the psalms lies in the fact that they speak so clearly about our needs. What we need most of all, of course, is salvation. The covenant of grace (the promise of salvation) is a thread which weaves its way through every page of Scripture's rich tapestry, and especially so in the psalms. Little wonder that they bubble with excitement at the thought that, despite the enormity of our sins, God has found a way to save us.

'Blessed is he whose transgression is forgiven,
Whose sin is covered.
Blessed is the man to whom the Lord does not impute
 iniquity...'

(Ps. 32:1-2).

Wherever we are in the Old Testament, God is talking to us about his plan of salvation. The book of Psalms brings it into sharp focus. How did the apostles know that there should have been a resurrection? True, they had heard Jesus foretell the event often enough. But they had also learnt to expect it from their knowledge of Psalm 16 (Acts 2:24-28; cf. Ps. 16:8-11). And how did they know about Jesus' exaltation? The truth had been revealed to them in Psalm 110 (Acts 2:34-36; cf. Ps. 110:1). For a description of Calvary they had Psalm 2, which had taught them to expect that the princes would combine against the Lord's Anointed and the people would imagine a vain thing. Nevertheless, God would set his King upon the holy hill of Zion (Acts 4:25-26; cf. Ps. 2:1-2).

The psalms portray Christ as God's anointed King who comes to die in the place of sinners. They also show Christians how to live so as to please him. Life is filled with stress. One of the first lessons the apostle Paul learned as an active worker in God's kingdom was that as a Christian, one can expect 'many tribulations' (Acts 14:22). Whether our problem is depression, fear, persecution, or sickness, the psalms have something to say to us.

The psalms were written by men like us

Perhaps the most appealing thing of all about the psalms is the fact that they were written by men like David, Asaph and Moses. It is wonderful to know that God has taken up and used the lives of sinful men, like David, in astonishing ways.

We all need help to overcome fears, frustrations and failures. David was a man who 'wore his heart on his sleeve'. He tells us exactly how he feels, and so often we too feel just the same. The psalms help us to appreciate how God enabled men like David to live and work for him. If we are willing to learn, we too can be useful for God.

Stephen, when he was dying from lethal wounds received from his enemies, found help by quoting a psalm. 'Lord Jesus, receive my spirit,' he cried, following the example of David, who also had known how powerful the spirit of revenge could be (Ps. 31:5).

Little wonder, then, that godly folk who spend time reading the psalms experience that joy which makes the Christian life so rich and rewarding and better than any other life the world can offer.

The psalms reflect the whole of human experience

Augustine, Luther, C. H. Spurgeon and C. S. Lewis all published their reflections on the psalms. For me to add to that number seems pretentious. I therefore need to explain myself!

I must confess that the psalms have not always been as rewarding to me as they are now. The apostle Peter makes the most startling admission in what may well have been the last letter he wrote before his cruel execution: 'Our beloved brother Paul, according to the wisdom given to him, has written to you, as also in all his epistles, speaking in them of these things, in which are some things hard to understand ...' (2 Peter 3:15-16). Not all the Bible is immediately accessible.

The world of the psalms reveals a variety of situations and demands a maturity of response that is often foreign to the young believer. Not every Christian has plumbed the depths experienced by the psalmist. Some of the passages, for example, the notorious imprecatory psalms, where the psalmist invokes curses on his enemies, are difficult to understand. That is why I have 'grown late' into the psalms.

At one level, the psalms have an immediate appeal for any Christian, but they also reflect a deeper reality — that known by a man who has travelled into areas we have only wondered at from a distance and who has experienced greater heights and depths of happiness and heartache, fellowship and fear, contentment and consternation, peace and provocation than many of us will ever know.

That is not to say that the psalms are therefore too remote from our world; they are not. It is true that some of the thoughts expressed by the psalmists are difficult for us to enter into, yet every Christian knows something of their emotions. There is not a spiritual experience that we face about which the book of Psalms does not have something to teach us. The psalms are, to use Calvin's imagery, the mirror of our spiritual lives.

A glance at the Contents page will show that I have chosen just ten psalms. This selection is a little arbitrary! It reflects, quite simply, ten psalms which have 'spoken to me' over the last few years.

Current studies in the psalms have been helpful in defining the varies types, or genres, of psalms.[6] Generally speaking they may be said to belong to one of the following categories:

the *hymn*, celebrating God's character;
the *lament*, giving expression to the pain and distress of
    someone in trouble;
the *psalm of remembrance*, recalling how God has
    worked in the past in keeping with his covenant
    promises;
the *psalm of confidence,* celebrating the victory of faith;

the *psalm of entreaty*, focusing on an extended prayer of
the psalmist;
the *wisdom psalm*, focusing particularly upon the
provision of God's Word to help us live so as to please
him;
the *kingship psalm*, celebrating the exaltation and
sovereign rule of Christ.

It is not always possible to define precisely the category into
which a particular psalm may fall. These are only guidelines to help
us group together some of the psalms.

Since one of the aims of this book is to help Christians in trouble,
I have included two *laments* (Ps. 22; 54). The pain felt by the
psalmist here (and in Psalm 22 by Christ himself) is a reminder to
us that, however bad we may feel, there is one who has gone this way
before us. The way out of the spiritual depression that can so often
accompany trials is to learn to praise God *despite* them. Thus
Psalms 5, 30 and 56 are psalms of thanksgiving designed to help
us sing to God in the midst of our troubles.

Psalm 71 is a psalm of confidence and trust as old age ap-
proaches relentlessly. I am persuaded that many are more troubled
by the ageing process than they are willing to admit. This psalm has
a reassuring quality that is particularly helpful.

Psalm 25 is an example of entreaty; learning how to pray is
something we have to return to again and again. If we could pray like
this, our spiritual lives would be transformed!

Psalm 119 is the Bible's own majestic statement about being
wise for God. And here I need to explain my method a little. Psalm
119 is too long to be taken in one bite. For my part, I think the Holy
Spirit has given us this psalm so that we may dip into it almost at
random and still get the message. In order to help the flow of the
book I have interspersed sections on this magnificent psalm
throughout the book. In doing so, I may inadvertently have helped
someone to see that returning frequently to this psalm will keep us
on the narrow path of obedience to our great Saviour. I trust so.

When Joseph was told by the angel to name Mary's son 'Jesus',
'because he will save his people from their sins' (Matt. 1:21), it was
in fulfilment of Psalm 130:8. Knowing the 'Jesus' of Psalm 130, and
the salvation he offers, is life's greatest treasure.

In commenting on these psalms my aim is to encourage you to take up some of the other psalms and 'live' with them for a while as I have done here. If you do, I assure you that you are in for an enriching experience.

Psalm 5

'Give ear to my words, O Lord,
Consider my meditation.
Give heed to the voice of my cry,
My King and my God,
For to you I will pray.
My voice you shall hear in the morning, O Lord;
In the morning I will direct it to you,
And I will look up.

For you are not a God who takes pleasure in wickedness,
Nor shall evil dwell with you.
The boastful shall not stand in your sight;
You hate all workers of iniquity.
You shall destroy those who speak falsehood;
The Lord abhors the bloodthirsty and deceitful man.

But as for me, I will come into your house in the multitude
    of your mercy;
In fear of you I will worship toward your holy temple.
Lead me, O Lord, in your righteousness because of my
    enemies;
Make your way straight before my face.

For there is no faithfulness in their mouth;
Their inward part is destruction;
Their throat is an open tomb;
They flatter with their tongue.
Pronounce them guilty, O God!
Let them fall by their own counsels;
Cast them out in the multitude of their transgressions,
For they have rebelled against you.

But let all those rejoice who put their trust in you;
Let them ever shout for joy, because you defend them;
Let those also who love your name
Be joyful in you.
For you, O Lord, will bless the righteous;
With favour you will surround him as with a shield.'

1.
'It's going to be one of those days...'

Psalm 5

Every night I carefully put all my troubles to bed and make sure they are all fast asleep — until, that is, I turn out the light. Then, like naughty children, they wake up again and make a nuisance of themselves.

I guess we all know something about sleepless nights. My own solution is to read. The problem, however, is the morning after! Sometimes I think it might have been better if I had not slept at all!

David had that problem. In 'the morning psalm' he says,

'I lay me down and slept;
I awoke, for the Lord sustained me'

(Ps. 3:5).

True, there seems to be no hint of insomnia in those lines. But just two psalms further on he tells us that there are mornings when things are not so calm and peaceful, which suggests to me that the night before had been stormy too.

'My voice you shall hear in the morning, O Lord;
In the morning I will direct it to you,
And I will look up...

The boastful shall not stand in your sight;
You hate all workers of iniquity.
You shall destroy those who speak falsehood;
The Lord abhors the bloodthirsty and deceitful man...
For there is no faithfulness in their mouth;
Their inward part is destruction;

> Their throat is an open tomb;
> They flatter with their tongue.
> Pronounce them guilty, O God!
> Let them fall by their own counsels;
> Cast them out in the multitude of their transgressions,
> For they have rebelled against you'
>
>   (Ps.5:3,5-6,9-10).

The day hasn't even started yet, and David is preoccupied with his enemies! I can just hear him muttering to himself, 'It's going to be one of those days!'

His morning devotions are full of worries about evil men. As I was saying, David strikes me as a man who has had a restless night! Perhaps you have had mornings like that; when you wondered how you were going to cope with the rest of the day. That's where this psalm can help: it is a morning prayer for protection.

Picking up the main lines of thought in the psalm, we can readily see three lines of help for troubled minds.

A listening ear

Did you notice what David says in the second verse? 'Give heed to the voice of my cry...' He wants the Lord to hear not just his prayer, but the very intonations in his voice. Why?

Think of it this way. Mothers are wonderful. They can discern the needs of their little babies just from the sound of their voices. There is a particular cry that means that Johnny is just waking up; one that means he's hungry, or that he just wants to be picked up; and there's one which signals real distress. Wise mothers, for their own sake (and for that of their babies) will learn to distinguish between when they need to rush over and pick the child up and when they can hang on for a minute or two.

Perhaps your line of expertise is another kind of 'baby' — the car! I'm always astonished when certain people can detect a faulty transmission just by the sound the engine makes when changing gear. I remember a good friend once saying about a car I used to own, which at the time was making a noise reminiscent of a sewing machine, 'It's the tappets.' I vividly recall being ashamed, not even knowing that my car had 'tappets'!

Just like a mother with her child, or a mechanic with his car, God can discern the needs of his children just from the sound they make. When David begins the psalm by saying, 'Consider my meditation' (the New International Version has 'groaning'), he uses an onomatopoeic word which in the Hebrew sounds extraordinarily like the muttering of an infant who cannot quite put words together.

I have had several long conversations with little children which have only made sense to me through a mother's interpretation. Unintelligible mutterings make perfect sense to those who are used to hearing them. So it is with our God. Morning devotions can be difficult, particularly after a sleepless night. In times of stress and tiredness it is hard to pray. But it is altogether wonderful to know that the Lord always knows our voice. He recognizes when we are tired, or confused, or when we are hurt: 'All my longings lie open before you, O Lord; my sighing is not hidden from you' (Ps. 38:9, NIV). And he knows just what we need!

Take it to the Lord in prayer!

Worries — we all have them; there's little point in denying it. But what to do with them?

David knew what to do with worries: he took them to the Lord.

'My voice you shall hear in the morning, O Lord;
In the morning I will direct it to you,
And I will look up.
But as for me, I will come into your house in the multitude
    of your mercy;
In fear of you I will worship toward your holy temple'
(vv. 3,7).

William Law, the eighteenth-century writer and moralist whose book *A Serious Call to a Devout and Holy Life* influenced the lives of the Wesleys, Whitefield and Henry Martyn, once wrote, 'He who has learned to pray has learned the greatest secret of a holy and a happy life.' And he was right! Prayer is God's greatest gift to his children.

According to one of those 'newsy' articles in a Saturday supplement, President Bush's children have access to their father day or night. The President of the United States may be dealing with a crisis in the Middle East, or the drugs problem in Latin America, or a million other matters affecting his own country, but he always has time for his children. The mind boggles as to all the things that occupy the mind of the great God, but he always has time for each one of his children, and it is always what is often called these days 'quality' time.

One of James Herriot's novels relating the lives of those veterinary folk from Yorkshire, *All Creatures Great and Small*, tells of the time Siegfried and James are left alone, their wives having gone to London for a week. Finding their respective homes quiet and lonely, they decide to move in with each other. 'It will be wonderful,' Siegfried says, 'just like old times when we used to spend long evenings in conversation around the fireside.' But they discover to their shame that they have lost the art of communication, and a television set is brought in to relieve the tedium.

Sometimes we discover the same in our relationship with God. To neglect communion with him is to neglect the most precious thing we have. Prayer, when you think about it, is knowing that we have a secure relationship with God and that we can address him in the knowledge that he cares and has the power to help us.

David had access to God. That is a surprising thing when we recall what he has already said in verse 4: 'For you are not a God who takes pleasure in wickedness, nor shall evil dwell with you.' I know that he is thinking here in terms of God's enemies: so long as they remain such, they shall never find access into his presence. But we are all enemies of God by nature. Even David is no exception to this!

Paul makes that very point in Romans 5:10. In fact, when David goes on to describe the mouths of God's enemies as resembling the inside of a sepulchre (v. 9), we find Paul applying the same image to every individual on the face of the earth (Rom. 3:13). As Thomas Boston said in *Human Nature in its Fourfold State*, 'The finest and nicest piece of the workmanship of heaven, if once the Creator's image upon it be defaced by sin, God can and will dash in pieces in his wrath, unless satisfaction be made to justice, and that image be restored; neither of which the sinner himself can do.'[1]

So how is it that David finds access and assurance in God's presence? The answer lies in verse 7: 'I will come into your house in the multitude of your mercy.' We have no natural right to come to God. Sin has formed a barrier between us and God. But God has found a way to forgive while at the same time remaining true to himself as a holy and righteous God who cannot let sin go unpunished (Rom. 3:26). He sent his only begotten Son to pay the price of redemption for sinners and bring them into fellowship with himself. That is why Paul says it is through the blood of Christ that we have access to the Father (Eph. 2:18). This is what David means by 'mercy' in verse 7.

It is interesting to note that in the third verse the translators have found it difficult to express just what David is saying. The Authorized Version refers to his 'prayer'. The word 'prayer' is in italics because it is not there in the Hebrew. Literally, the verse reads something like this: 'In the morning I make preparations for you and watch.' This phrase 'to make preparations' is in fact the very expression used for laying the fire for a burnt offering (Lev. 1:7-9; possibly for the morning sacrifice, cf. Exod. 29:42). The only way David could come to God was by way of a sacrifice offered up in his place. It is the same for us: God has reconciled us to himself through Jesus Christ (2 Cor. 5:18).

> There is no other good enough
> To pay the price of sin;
> He only must unlock the gates
> Of heaven, and let us in.

> (Cecil Frances Alexander).

Looking for answers

What David wants most of all is justice (v.10). This is something we find frequently in the psalms. Evil men are prospering; the godly are having a hard time of it. Where is God? Why doesn't he come down and show himself as the powerful and just God that he is? Why doesn't he consume them all in his wrath? Why am I being persecuted when I'm trying so hard to follow him? It is the kind of feeling that every Christian has at some time or another.

If you read quickly through Psalm 73 you will get some idea of just how irritated the psalmists could become when they saw wicked and ungodly people prospering. Until he comes to his senses (something which he does halfway through the psalm) the writer confesses that he was on the point of giving up (cf. 73:2). Surely, he thought, there's no point to it all if God treats his children like this! But there is a point. The wicked will one day receive their just deserts, if not just now (Ps. 73:18-20; 1 Thess. 5:3).

So why do Christians have all this trouble to face? Several things have to be borne in mind if we are ever to make sense of suffering.

Firstly, the whole world is cursed and out of joint. Creation, of which we are a part, is subject to 'futility', a failure to achieve (Rom. 8:20,22). Just as death is part of this curse, so are all the things that bring about death. Christians, not yet in glory, are not promised exemption from this general curse.

Secondly, we are told that just as our Saviour suffered, so must his followers (Heb. 12:3). Experiencing pain is to be expected, for the devil continues to throw all he can against Christ and those who claim to be his.

Thirdly, often our suffering is God's way of training us, bringing us up short and making us more dependent on him and less on ourselves. By so doing he makes us more useful (2 Cor. 12:7-10; Heb. 12:2).

Fourthly, we are always to remember that however much we suffer, it is never in proportion to what we deserve. Keeping that in mind will keep us from getting angry with God.

Concern for justice, so long as it doesn't end up as self-pity, or ambition, is perfectly laudable. What is significant for us to remember is that David took his concerns to God in prayer. He poured out his heart to God, telling him just how he felt. You and I must do the same with our cares. But then what? That is where this psalm is so helpful.

Chariots of fire!

Take a look at verse 12: 'For you, O Lord, will bless the righteous; with favour you will surround him as with a shield.' Did you ever watch one of those 'cowboys and Indians' films where the bedraggled band of men with their wagons awake to the sound of Indians howling and baying outside. 'It's no use, boss,' someone says. 'We're completely surrounded.'

'God will surround me,' David reminds himself, using a word that is used on only one other occasion in the Old Testament. This is in 1 Samuel 23:26, where Saul's army is closing in on David when suddenly the Philistines invade the land and Saul has to flee away to see to it. At the same time that Saul is surrounding David, God is surrounding him to protect him.

I must confess to having favourite passages of Scripture, ones I often repeat in sermons and at hospital bedsides. One such is the story of Elisha and his servant. The Syrians were making predatory incursions into Israel, only to be thwarted by Elisha's prophetic warnings to the King of Israel. The only solution for the Syrians was to have Elisha destroyed.

I can just see that poor servant, rubbing his eyes first thing in the morning as he goes out to the plains of Dothan to do what he has to do. Up on the hills he sees them — hundreds of them! Warriors from Syria! How big they look first thing in the morning! I can hear him saying to Elisha, 'Alas, my master! What shall we do?' (2 Kings 6:15).

Elisha did not panic because he could see something the servant couldn't: the chariots of fire! 'Do not fear, for those who are with us are more than those who are with them,' he replied. Now there we see faith at work. Elisha, just like David after his morning devotions, could detect, in the midst of the trouble, the encircling hand of God all around him.

That explains why, at the very beginning of the psalm, David is watching for God to work. Some translations have rendered it, 'I will look up' (v. 3). The word he uses means 'to watch'. That is what later prophets would do: announce God's message and then go and watch for it to occur (Isa. 21:6,8; Micah 7:7; Hab. 2:1). That is how we are to pray. 'Watch and pray,' said Jesus on several occasions (Matt. 24:42; Mark 13:33; 14:38).

The psalmist describes in Psalm 130 how he waits on the Lord with more eagerness than a watchman in his tower waits for the first signs of dawn so that his shift might end and another night free of trouble be over.

How many times have you prayed and then forgotten all about it? You haven't watched for his answers. Every day God fills our lives with answers to prayer if only we open our eyes to see what he is doing. All we can think about is the trouble that God has allowed to come our way, but can you imagine just how many things God has delivered us from? That is why David finishes this psalm with a call for Christians to rejoice. God is our defender (v.11). He surrounds his children 'as with a shield' (v.12). No matter how hard the difficulties may seem to be, his shield has taken most of the blow out of it.

Remember what I wrote earlier about God knowing the very sound of your cry? He hears even your groans: 'All my longings lie open before you, O Lord; my sighing is not hidden from you' (Ps. 38:9, NIV). He delights to hear you praise him, too. So what about it? Let him hear you praise him today. Think of all the things that have happened to show you that he loves you, and praise him. Then go on praising him for the things that you cannot think about.

And those enemies? Open your eyes. Look—the chariots of fire!

Psalm 25

'To you, O Lord, I lift up my soul.
O my God, I trust in you;
Let me not be ashamed;
Let not my enemies triumph over me.
Indeed, let no one who waits on you be ashamed;
Let those be ashamed who deal treacherously without
   cause.

Show me your ways, O Lord;
Teach me your paths.
Lead me in your truth and teach me,
For you are the God of my salvation;
On you I wait all the day.

Remember, O Lord, your tender mercies and your
   lovingkindnesses,
For they have been from of old.
Do not remember the sins of my youth, nor my
   transgressions;
According to your mercy remember me,
For your goodness' sake, O Lord.

Good and upright is the Lord;
Therefore he teaches sinners in the way.
The humble he guides in justice,
And the humble he teaches his way.
All the paths of the Lord are mercy and truth,
To such as keep his covenant and his testimonies.
For your name's sake, O Lord,
Pardon my iniquity, for it is great.

Who is the man that fears the Lord?
Him shall he teach in the way he chooses.
He himself shall dwell in prosperity,
And his descendants shall inherit the earth.
The secret of the Lord is with those who fear him,
And he will show them his covenant.
My eyes are ever toward the Lord,
For he shall pluck my feet out of the net.

Turn yourself to me, and have mercy on me,
For I am desolate and afflicted.
The troubles of my heart have enlarged;
Oh, bring me out of my distresses!
Look on my affliction and my pain,
And forgive all my sins.
Consider my enemies, for they are many;
And they hate me with cruel hatred.
Oh, keep my soul, and deliver me;
Let me not be ashamed, for I put my trust in you.
Let integrity and uprightness preserve me,
For I wait for you.

Redeem Israel, O God,
Out of all their troubles!'

2.
Help for the mind: Christian meditation

Psalm 25

Whatever happened to Maharishi Mahesh Yogi? In the sixties his name was on every university notice-board. He was the one who made Transcendental Meditation (TM for short) a household phrase. His followers were noted for their somewhat weird, unconventional appearance. I remember hearing some of his more devoted followers repeating mantras (words or phrases repeated over and over again). It is a sign of just how quickly fashion and tastes change that today's young people will hardly even recognize his name.

In the first chapter we saw how Psalm 5 teaches us to 'look up' in times of trouble. Learning to do just that requires that we walk closely with God. To do this we must learn something about spiritual meditation.

Psalm 25 touches on the theme of meditation — not TM but CM, that is, Christian meditation![1] It does not actually use the word 'meditation', but throughout the psalm there are the signs of a man engaged in spiritual meditation. The psalm opens with the words: 'To you, O Lord, I lift up my soul.' We are meant to imagine someone looking into the 'face' of God in adoration and submissiveness. Here is someone whose gaze is fixed wholly upon the Lord, concentrating upon him in such a way that all else fades into the background. It is the same order of thought that we find in verse 15: 'My eyes are ever toward the Lord, for he shall pluck my feet out of the net.'

Meditating on the Lord is God's way of helping us out of some of our troubles. As we focus on him, our problems sometimes seem much less than we initially imagine.

If prayer is talking to God, then meditation is thinking about God in his presence. I add 'in his presence' quite deliberately for meditation is not something abstract and detached. It is not the student shut away in his room pouring over his books, but a little boy who sits in his father's lap and looks at, and listens adoringly to, the astonishing knowledge and abilities he perceives in his father.

Just take a look, for example, at how the psalmist almost 'mutters' to himself about the nature and character of God in verses 8-10 and 12-15, and you will see what I mean. This is what spiritual meditation is: reflecting aloud upon the nature of God.

This is something we often find in the psalms. The Psalter opens this way:

'Blessed is the man
Who walks not in the counsel of the ungodly,
Nor stands in the path of sinners,
Nor sits in the seat of the scornful;
But his delight is in the law of the Lord,
And in his law he meditates day and night'

(Ps. 1:1,2).

Meditation will help us deal with anger: 'Be angry, and do not sin. Meditate within your heart on your bed, and be still' (Ps. 4:4).

Meditation is to be part of our morning and evening devotions (Ps. 5:1-2; 63:6; 77:6). Eight times we are told in Psalm 119 that meditating on God's law will help us grow and be strong (vv. 15, 23, 27, 48, 78, 97, 99, 148). In short, meditation will 'make us glad' (Ps. 104:34).

Clearly, serious-minded Christians will take meditation seriously! In fact, the Hebrew word used for meditation here in Psalm 25 means 'to mutter' and is used to describe the growling of a lion and the cooing of a dove (Isa. 31:4; 59:11). What the psalmist seems to have in mind is the repetition of words.

'Muttering' Bible words, especially in days before pocket Bibles existed, was about the only way God's Word could stick in the mind. Meditation, then, need not necessarily be done in silence! 'And my tongue shall speak of your righteousness and of your praise all the day long' (Ps. 35:28).

Psalm 25 is one of those psalms written (more or less) around the framework of the Hebrew alphabet, each new line beginning with a new Hebrew character. (We shall come across this again as we glance at Psalm 119 throughout this book.) Psalms written this way were meant to help in the memorization of their contents. Meditation and memorization go hand in hand, of course. God intends us to use his Word this way.

Several dominant themes emerge in the psalm: the pressure of enemies all around us, the need for God to guide us and the burden of the guilt of sin. All of us know these things only too well in our lives. This psalm, then, recommends meditation to help us through the difficulties of life. Taking the psalm as a whole, four lessons seem to come into focus.

Balance

One particular feature of the psalm is the way that the psalmist sandwiches prayer and meditation. I must admit to a certain fondness for a good gateau, especially the sort with several layers of filling! Psalm 25 is a bit like that: a five-layer cake of prayer (1-7), meditation (8-10), prayer (11), meditation (12-15) and prayer (16-22).

Meditation is not giving free rein to your imagination, nor is it reading your Bible for beautiful thoughts. Meditation is a discipline. Spiritual meditation needs to be worked at! The natural course of our thoughts is not spiritual at all, but they can be encouraged by the help of the Holy Spirit to ascend up to heaven. Just as water naturally descends, John Owen once observed, it can, nevertheless be made to go up through clever use of pressure.[2] Psalm 25 seems to tell us, more by example than anything it specifically says, that prayer and meditation go hand in hand. There ought to be a balance of prayer and meditation in our lives.

In the Protestant tradition there has, rightly, been an emphasis upon petition rather than contemplation. People who, after all, know their God will talk to him freely, as children do to their fathers. Those who do not know God will only feel a sense of mystery and strangeness when they pray. For such, silence speaks louder than words.

But we are mistaken if we think that there is no place for meditation. Psalm 119, as we shall see, is a meditation from beginning to end. The entire psalm is about God's law. Over and over again the psalmist turns a thought around in his mind, shining light at it from every possible angle.

Psalms like these are not meant for reading at speed! They teach us how to take a precious truth and chew on it, extracting all the juices slowly and carefully: 'I will meditate on your precepts, and contemplate your ways ' (Ps.119:15).

Repetition

The pivotal point of the psalm occurs at verse 11: 'For your name's sake, O Lord, pardon my iniquity, for it is great.' It is a prayer invoking the name of God, a name which, for the psalmist, speaks of mercy and forgiveness. This leads us to the second lesson, repeating ourselves in prayer.

Sometimes, when leading a prayer meeting, I have suggested that prayers should be kept short. The reason I say this is, partly, because some young Christians feel almost intimidated by long prayers, saying to themselves, 'Oh, I could never pray like that!' Young Christians need to be encouraged to pray out loud, and short prayers, with a broken heart and a contrite spirit, are the best way of doing it. After all, it was the Pharisees who made long prayers: 'But when you pray, do not use vain repetitions as the heathen do. For they think that they will be heard for their many words' (Matt. 6:7).

But the main reason I sometimes encourage short prayers is because lengthy prayers can become repetitive. Jesus warned about this tendency in the passage we have just quoted. Repetition in itself is not wrong. What Jesus condemns is 'vain' repetitions. There were some who believed that repeating something over several times possessed some inherent magical power. Jesus would have no part in such superstition.

In Psalm 25 the psalmist repeats himself three times:

'Do not remember the sins of my youth,
    nor my transgressions;
According to your mercy remember me,
For your goodness' sake, O Lord'

(v.7).

'For your name's sake, O Lord,
Pardon my iniquity, for it is great'

(v.11).

'Look on my affliction and my pain,
And forgive all my sins'

(v.18).

Why this repetition? Whenever I have been in a meeting, especially one where the business has been particularly interesting, I will come home and tell my wife all about it. First of all, I have to give a short version so as to give her the whole gist of it. Then comes a more detailed version with all the various nuances and colour added. Then, perhaps the next day, a significant detail is recalled and again the story is retold with this particular emphasis added. We all do this sort of thing, telling each other something that is on our minds, and we tend to repeat ourselves — sometimes for emphasis, sometimes because we can't help ourselves!

The psalmist wants forgiveness. It is a burden to him. And he cannot be content with just saying it once! He simply cannot help telling God about it, over and over again. It is all right with God when we repeat ourselves in prayer when our hearts are so troubled about something.

Nor is this the only thing he is burdened about: twice he says that he 'waits upon the Lord' (vv. 5,21). This introduces the third lesson: learning to wait in silence upon God.

Silence

The word translated 'wait' in this psalm is sometimes given a slightly different connotation. In the New American Standard Version, for example, the same word, is translated this way in Psalm 62:1: 'My soul waits in silence for God only.' To 'wait' can mean 'to be silent before God'.

We have already seen that meditation need not be done in silence. Old Testament saints, it seems, repeated God's Word aloud so as to remember it. What the psalmist means in Psalm 62 is quite different. He is speaking there, not so much about audibility as humility. It is something like what Paul says in Romans 3. There he is arguing about the universality of sin. The law, God's moral law, condemns everyone. The whole point of the law is that no one can boast in God's sight. Paul puts it like this: 'Now we know that whatever the law says, it says to those who are under the law, that every mouth may be stopped, and all the world may become guilty before God' (Rom. 3:19).

One of the things God's law does is to shut us up! Standing in God's presence, we have nothing to boast about. All we can do is praise him for the greatness of his salvation in Jesus Christ! This is what the psalmist does here: 'For you are the God of my salvation' (v.5). Then immediately he says, 'On you I wait all the day.' He waits on God to save him. He cannot save himself. His mouth is stopped. He has no righteousness to offer that would be acceptable to a holy God. Instead all his hope is in the Lord. He looks up to God in faith and hope for mercy and deliverance. It is an Old Testament way of saying that the way to be right with God is through faith in his Son Jesus Christ.

The psalmist trusts in God in the fullest sense — expecting complete deliverance through all the trials and problems of life until God brings him to himself (v.2). His mouth is closed to grumbling and discontentment. He waits 'in silence' upon the Lord, trusting him to do all things well for him.

There is also a fourth lesson and it is that in Christ we are in fellowship with a covenant God, and if we obey him we can expect great things.

Promise

Why do we trust God? What encouragements are there for us to do so? The answer lies in the somewhat difficult fourteenth verse: 'The secret of the Lord is with those who fear him; and he will show them his covenant.'

What is a covenant? Quite simply it is a bond, in which God binds himself to us, pledging to make all his resources available to us for our blessing. When a man and a woman marry, they enter into a covenant, promising faithfulness, giving themselves to each other entirely, without reservation.

So the Lord (this is God's 'covenant name') promises here to be our loving Husband, faithful for now and eternity. Note that in verse

2 the psalmist comes to the heart of things when he calls God 'my God'. That is what the covenant is all about. It is God saying, 'I will be your God; and you will be my people.' No matter how hard things get, God is still our God. That is a promise!

Psalms like this one are meant to help us through difficult times. They are God's provision for times of trouble. God's covenant is designed to remind us of how God's dealings with us are predictable. Whereas the gods of the nations were irrational and capricious, Israel's God was utterly different. Jehovah (Yahweh, as he was known to the Jews) has spoken. He has shown us something of himself and the way he deals with us. Once spoken in covenant, God's word is his oath (Heb. 6:16-18). Let's explore a little what this might mean.

1. God forgives (vv.7,11)

God freely forgives all those who trust in his word of promise. In the Old Testament, God's promises pointed to the coming of his Son. All the ceremonial ritual pointed to his coming. The law, which for ever accused, drove men and women to the Christ of promise (Heb. 9:15). This particular guilt-ridden sinner in Psalm 25 found grace in the eyes of God.

We too can know that same grace of God if we bring our sins to Jesus Christ, and ask forgiveness. Even though we are already Christians, having already been justified and made right with God, we still need daily cleansing. Jesus taught us in the 'model prayer' to say every day, 'Forgive us our debts as we forgive our debtors.'

I was once asked why it is that I, so often, end my public prayers with the words: 'and forgive us our sins'. Are we not already forgiven if we are Christians? Why do we ask God to keep on forgiving us? The answer lies, I think, in distinguishing God as Judge from God as Father. As Christians we are forgiven. The judgement of God, which our sins deserve, has already been executed upon Jesus Christ. Since we have been justified, our sins no longer threaten our legal relationship to God. But God is also our Father. God's children, when they sin, need not worry that he will throw them out of his house; yet things will not be right until they have the humility to go and say 'sorry'. And we need to remember that whatever sins we may be conscious of, they are far worse than we ever imagine! Archbishop Ussher prayed, when he was dying, 'Forgive most of all my sins of omission.'

2. *God guides, guards and delivers*

'The humble he guides in justice, and the humble he teaches his
way' (v. 9); 'Oh, keep my soul, and deliver me; let me not be
ashamed, for I put my trust in you' (v. 20). Providence, the way God
deals with us in our lives, is to be a constant theme of our meditation.
'The Lord's voice cries to the city — wisdom shall see your name:
"Hear the Rod! Who has appointed it?"' (Micah 6:9). God would
have us be content with our lot (Phil. 4:6).

The psalmist is confident that God will deliver him (v.20).
Confidence about the future, no matter what may happen, is what
faith is all about. This is what helped our Lord endure the cross (Heb.
12:2), and Stephen the painful death by stoning (Acts 7:54-58). John
Owen, writing on the subject of 'spiritual-mindedness', compared
looking to heaven to gazing at the sun. 'He that looks steadily on the
sun,' he wrote, 'although he cannot bear the lustre of its beams fully,
yet his sight is so affected with it that when he calls off his eyes from
it, he can see nothing as it were of the things about him; they are all
dark to him. And he who looks steadily in his contemplations on
things above, eternal things, though he cannot comprehend their
glory, yet a veil will be cast by it on all the desirable beauties of
earthly things, and take off his affections from them.'[3]

John Owen's words proved right for Margaret Maclachlan.
During the 'killing times' when brave Covenanters refused to obey
the king before God, two godly women stand out: Margaret
Maclachlan and Margaret Wilson, the 'Wigtown Martyrs'.
Maclachlan was a girl of eighteen, and Margaret Wilson a woman
of seventy. In April 1685, they were sentenced to be 'tied to stakes
fixed within the flood-mark in the Water of Blednoch, near
Wigtown, where the sea flows at high water, there to be drowned'.
The sentence was carried out on 11 May 1685. The elder of 'the two
Margarets' was set lower down the river, so that the younger might
see her struggles, and her death, and hopefully 'repent'. It proved not
to be so. Having witnessed the death of her friend, as the salty waters
reached her neck Margaret Maclachlan was heard to sing the
twenty-fifth Psalm, with the words:

My sins and faults of youth,
Do thou, O Lord, forget;

After thy mercies, think on me,
And for thy goodness great.

3. God befriends his people

The secret of the Lord is with those who fear him, and he will show
them his covenant' (v.14). This is a difficult verse. What it seems to
mean is that the Lord confides in those who fear him. He takes them
into his confidence as friends. It is a little similar to what happened
to Abraham when God asked, 'Shall I hide from Abraham what I am
doing?' (Gen.18:17). Jesus also said, 'You are my friends if you do
whatever I command you' (John 15:14).

He is the friend of sinners. Think about it! We tend to make
friends with people because they please us in some way. We find in
them something worthy of friendship. Our Lord, on the other hand,
makes us his friends despite the fact that we are sinners and therefore
enemies of God by nature. Such is the love of God.

We began by noting that this psalm is a wonderful example of the
balance of prayer and meditation. What we have found is that
meditation, whereby our minds are engaged in thought on the
meaning of Scripture, provides the impetus for, and the content of
prayer. As Philip Henry (the father of Matthew Henry) once said,
'Meditation keeps out Satan. It increases knowledge, it inflames
love, it works patience, it promotes prayer, it evidences sincerity.'

A psalm such as this one will help you in your troubles!

Psalm 119, part 1

'Blessed are the undefiled in the way,
Who walk in the law of the Lord!
Blessed are those who keep his testimonies,
Who seek him with the whole heart!
They also do no iniquity;
They walk in his ways.
You have commanded us
To keep your precepts diligently.
Oh, that my ways were directed
To keep your statutes!
Then I would not be ashamed,
When I look into all your commandments.
I will praise you with uprightness of heart,
When I learn your righteous judgements.
I will keep your statutes;
Oh, do not forsake me utterly! '

(vv. 1-8).

3.
God's alphabet psalm

Psalm 119, part 1

Bible quizzes invariably ask the question: 'What is the longest psalm in the Bible?' The answer, as every child knows, is Psalm 119. It is ten times the length of the average psalm.

Its layout is a little special: 176 verses divided into twenty-two sections of eight verses each, with each line of each section beginning with a letter from the Hebrew alphabet (which has only twenty-two characters). It is, like Psalms 9, 10, 25, 34, 37, 111, 112 and 145, an acrostic psalm.

My children are particularly fond of 'Alphabet Spaghetti'. (It's the novelty of spelling out something with your dinner!) Most children begin their literary lives with plastic or wooden alphabet shapes. It is the same with this psalm. Written with the young in mind (cf.v. 9), Psalm 119 is the Holy Spirit's teaching aid, God's alphabet psalm.

Apart from verse 122, every single line alludes to God's Word in some shape or form. Psalm 119 is a psalm in celebration of the Bible. As it so happens, it occurs almost exactly halfway through the Bible (falling, at least in my edition, at page 699 of a version having 1393 pages!). It is as though the Holy Spirit were saying by way of a reminder, halfway through his written revelation, that God has spoken; the wise should sit up and take heed.

Christians in every age have found the psalm of incalculable profit. Jonathan Edwards' testimony is typical: 'I know of no part of the Holy Scriptures where the nature and evidences of true and sincere godliness are so fully and largely insisted on and delineated, as in the 119th Psalm.'[1]

'Give me understanding'

To suggest that Psalm 119 is a psalm about wisdom may sound an exaggeration when we discover that only one verse in the entire psalm actually refers to wisdom: 'You, through your commandments, make me wiser than my enemies; for they are ever with me' (v. 98). But that would be to miss a vital clue in the psalm. The clue is in the word 'understanding'. Here are some of the ways the psalmist cries out for understanding:

'Make me understand the way of your precepts;
So shall I meditate on your wondrous works'

(v.27).

'Give me understanding, and I shall keep your law;
Indeed, I shall observe it with my whole heart'

(v.34).

'Your hands have made me and fashioned me;
Give me understanding, that I may learn your
     commandments'
              (v. 73; cf. vv. 79, 100, 104, 125, 130, 144 , 169).

Wisdom and understanding are marriage partners. The opening verses of the book of Proverbs tell us that the function of these wise sayings is to help us 'know wisdom and instruction, to perceive the words of understanding' (Prov. 1:2). Later on, Solomon says, 'How much better it is to get wisdom than gold! And to get understanding is to be chosen rather than silver' (Prov. 16:16).

Clearly, wisdom and understanding belong together. But what is it that these biblical writers want to know? John Calvin's answer is, by now, well known. In the opening lines of his *Institutes*, he suggested that 'Nearly all the wisdom we possess, that is to say, true and sound wisdom, consists of two parts: the knowledge of God and of ourselves.'[2]

To gain wisdom, we must know God. And the way we come to know God, and what he desires from us, is in his Word. It is also the answer of this epic psalm: the psalmist wants to understand God's Word so that he may keep it! What could be simpler than that? Jesus concludes his great sermon with a portrait of the wise man: he is the one who builds his house on solid foundations that will withstand the fiercest storms. He is the one who 'hears these sayings of mine, and does them' (Matt. 7:24-27).

The beatific vision

Like three other psalms (1, 32, 41) it begins with the word 'blessed'. This is the word Jesus used to declare his covenant benediction on those who live in the way he intends (Matt. 5:3-12). Like the Sermon on the Mount, the psalm is meant to be read in the context of the covenant: 'to bless' (like its negative 'to curse') is a covenant word. When the Israelites were reminded of the terms and conditions of God's covenantal dealings with them on the plains of Moab, God promised a series of blessings to those who were faithful to him, and warned of curses which the disobedient could expect (Deut. 27; 28).

The privilege which Adam and Eve had formerly known in the garden was to be restored to Abraham (Gen.1:28; 12:3). God blessed him, promising to be his God. He was to have his name changed from Abram to Abraham, 'the father of many', because he was to become the father of a large spiritual family that would know the Lord. Knowing God in restored fellowship through his Son, Jesus Christ, is what it means to be blessed.

Some have rightly suggested that the word 'blessed' means 'to be happy'. Psalm 119 is a psalm about being 'happy in Jesus'. As J. H. Sammis put it,

Trust and obey,
For there's no other way
To be happy in Jesus,
But to trust and obey.

Obeying God by taking a delight in his Word (vv.77, 92), is what this psalm is all about. The secret of a happy life is to trust and obey the Lord who reveals himself in the Scriptures. Psalm 119 is the Bible's own testimony to what the Reformers would summarize in one sentence as the Christian's chief concern: glorifying and enjoying God (Shorter Catechism: Question and Answer 1).

The answer of Psalm 119 to the question: 'How can I be happy?' is to say, over and over again, 'Live in his Word and let his Word live in you' (cf. vv.77, 92).

Jeremy Taylor, who was Bishop of Down and Connor during the reign of Charles II, wrote, 'God threatens terrible things if we are not happy.' Although Psalm 119 majors on the positive, refraining from spelling out in any detail the consequences of disobedience to the covenant life, the mere thought of it made the psalmist's heart tremble: 'My flesh trembles for fear of you, and I am afraid of your judgements' (v.120). Earlier, he had written a word of warning: 'You rebuke the proud — the cursed, who stray from your commandments' (v. 21). C. S. Lewis wrote in *The Last Battle*, 'There is a kind of happiness that makes you serious.' A happiness bordering on seriousness, not levity, is what Psalm 119 is anxious to talk about.

Three key-concepts open up the first section of the psalm.

Happiness lies in the way of holiness

If the Bible is clear about anything it is this: there is no ultimate satisfaction in a life of sin. 'Blessed are the undefiled in the way, who walk in the law of the Lord!' (v.1). Charles Bridges explains that by 'undefiled' (NIV 'blameless') the psalmist means 'not one who is without sin, but one who in the sincerity of his heart can say, "That which I do, I allow not" (Rom. 7:15).'[3]

A Christian is characterized, not by sinlessness, but by a desire to be free from sin. Several times, this point is made clear: 'Your word I have hidden in my heart, that I might not sin against you' (v.11); 'Let my heart be blameless ... that I may not be ashamed' (v. 80); 'I have restrained my feet from every evil way...' (v.101). They who are happy 'do no iniquity' (v. 3).

It is not that a Christian is sinless. In the very last verse the psalmist makes the point that he has just experienced a recovery from the power of sin in his life: 'I have gone astray like a lost sheep.' A similar testimony is given in verse 67: 'Before I was afflicted I went astray.'

Sinlessness is not part of the psalmist's experience. What the psalmist is saying is taken up by the apostle John, when he says, 'Whoever has been born of God does not sin' (1 John 3:9; cf. 3:6; 5:18). That John is not talking about sinless perfection is made abundantly clear in the opening chapter of his epistle: 'If we say that we have no sin, we deceive ourselves, and the truth is not in us' (1 John 1:8; cf. 3:8). What John and the psalmist are saying is that sin is no longer the dominating characteristic in the believer's life.

Paul makes the same point in his letter to the Romans, when he refers to Christians as having been 'set free from sin' (Rom. 6:22). 'Sin,' he asserts, 'shall not have dominion over you' (Rom. 6:14). There can be only one ruler in our lives at any one time. As the Puritan John Owen put it, 'Grace and sin may be in the same soul at the same time, but they cannot bear rule in the same soul at the same time.'[4]

When the question, 'Who is in charge?' is asked about a believer, the answer of Psalm 119 is 'the Word of God'. Robert Murray M'Cheyne prayed, 'Make me as holy as a saved sinner can be.' Psalm 119 urges us to pray the same prayer.

Happiness lies in the way of obedience to God's law

Some Christians are strangers to Psalm 119. It is a strange world to them. They insist that they 'are not under law, but under grace'; and when the psalmist rings the changes on God's law, to them he speaks a foreign language. Antinomianism, the belief that Christians have no duty to obey the law, is still a potent force in the Christian church. Try, for example, telling certain Christians that they have a duty to keep the Lord's Day holy and there will inevitably be some kind of reaction. Usually it comes in the form of a charge of 'legalism'. To insist on obedience is seriously to devalue the life of grace. So runs the charge.

The psalmist's frame of reference could hardly be more different. Like Psalm 19, Psalm 119 culls the Bible's legal vocabulary to make the point that God's law is a multi-faceted precious stone. Partly, this is because the psalm is poetry, and repetition of the same word would be bad form; but primarily, the reason lies in the need to show that God's law is wonderfully rich and varied, an expression of how God is in himself. As the Puritan Thomas Manton put it, commenting on Psalm 119, 'The original draft [of God's law] is in God himself.'[5]

Let us take a look at the psalm and we shall discover just how many different words are used to describe God's law.[6] Here are some of them:

'Law' (Torah). ' Blessed are the undefiled in the way, who walk in the law of the Lord' (v.1). This is the word used most often. Its

meaning is varied, referring to either the whole law, a single command or even the Scriptures (cf. John.15:25 and 1 Cor.14:21 which quote the Psalms and Prophets using the name 'Law'). It comes from a root meaning to 'project' or 'teach' and thus comes to mean whatever indicates God's will to man. Think of what a projector does: by throwing light on to a screen it helps us see things, people or places about which we might otherwise know nothing. God's law is similar: it projects his law to help us see better his will for our lives.

'Testimony' (+eduwth). 'Blessed are those who keep his testimonies' (v. 2). This usually refers to the tablets containing the summary of the law which were placed in the ark as a testimony, or witness, to the covenant between God and his people (Exod. 25:16-22). The word 'testimony' is at times almost synonymous with 'covenant' (e.g., Deut. 9:15).

'Precept' (piqqud). 'You have commanded us to keep your precepts diligently' (v.4). Literally, this word means a 'thing appointed', or a 'charge'. 'Precepts' are usually detailed, concrete instructions for specific situations (e.g., building a parapet around a two-storey building, Deut. 22:8). The word is drawn from the realm of an officer or overseer called upon to examine in detail. Think of an army officer examining in detail the uniform of a soldier on parade, and you will catch the gist of what the law does in our lives.

'Statute' (chuqqa). 'Oh, that my ways were directed to keep your statutes!' (v. 5). God's statutes are permanent. Once written down, they cannot be altered: 'Now go, write it before them on a tablet, and note [chuqqa] it on a scroll' (Isa. 30:8).

'Commandment' (mitsvah). 'Then I would not be ashamed, when I look into all your commandments' (v.6). The emphasis is upon authority. When God speaks no one can contradict him. His word is final. If the law states a matter, that is it. There is no basis for further enquiry.

'Judgement' (mishpat). 'I will praise you with uprightness of heart, when I learn your righteous judgements' (v. 7). Like 'precepts' *(piqqud)*, 'judgements' are specific applications of the law. Two

whole chapters are given over to this, each one beginning with, 'If this happens ... then...' (Exod. 21; 22).

'Word' (dabar). How can a young man cleanse his way? By taking heed according to your word' (v. 9). This is the most general term of all and refers to God's Word in whatever form it is found.

'Way' (derek). 'They also do no iniquity; they walk in his ways' (v. 3). Those who live in obedience to God's laws are said to walk in his 'way'. The word describes a person's lifestyle.[7]

In one way or another all these terms refer to God's Word— spoken, commanded and written. Since every word of Scripture is God's Word then Psalm 119 is the psalmist's own testimony in advance of what Paul would put more succinctly: 'All Scripture is given by inspiration of God, and is profitable for doctrine, for reproof, for correction, for instruction in righteousness' (2 Tim. 3:16).

Happiness means having a right relationship with our Bibles. If we are out of sorts here, everything else is sickened too. That is why the opening emphasis falls on memorizing (v. 7), keeping (vv. 2, 4, 5, 8), walking in (v. 1), looking into (v. 6) and delighting in his Word (vv. 14, 16).

Happiness lies in the way of fellowship with God

This is the psalm's third key-concept. The truly happy man finds his joy in a wholehearted walk with God (v. 2). The covenant promise that those who truly seek after God with all their hearts shall find him is underlined here, too (cf. Jer. 29:13).

Knowing God, sharing with him a life of fellowship and willing service, is what we were made for. Happiness comes in acknowledging it with enthusiasm.

Psalm 30

'I will extol you, O Lord, for you have lifted me up,
And have not let my foes rejoice over me.
O Lord my God, I cried out to you,
And you have healed me.
O Lord, you have brought my soul up from the grave;
You have kept me alive, that I should not go down to the pit.

Sing praise to the Lord, you saints of his,
And give thanks at the remembrance of his holy name.
For his anger is but for a moment,
His favour is for life;
Weeping may endure for a night,
But joy comes in the morning.

Now in my prosperity I said,
"I shall never be moved."
Lord, by your favour you have made my mountain stand
    strong;
You hid your face, and I was troubled.

I cried out to you, O Lord;
And to the Lord I made supplication:
"What profit is there in my blood,
When I go down to the pit?
Will the dust praise you?
Will it declare your truth?
Hear, O Lord, and have mercy on me;
Lord, be my helper!"

You have turned for me my mourning into dancing;
You have put off my sackcloth and clothed me with
    gladness,
To the end that my glory may sing praise to you and not be
    silent.
O Lord my God, I will give thanks to you for ever.'

4.
Help for the body: the healing touch

Psalm 30

Bishop John Hooper, English Reformer and martyr, was taken to the
Fleet prison, to a 'vile and stinking chamber', with nothing for his
bed but a 'little pad of straw' and 'a rotten covering'. During his
imprisonment he is said to have committed Psalm 30 to memory,
'for its lesson on patience and consolation at times when the mind
can take no understanding nor the heart any joy in God's promise'.
On 9 February 1555, he was burnt at the stake, his death protracted
for up to an hour by the greenness and insufficiency of the
materials.[1]

There was a time in David's life when he almost died and he
wasn't ready for it. However much Christians may speak about
being ready to die, and some do with obvious sincerity, few are
prepared for the *process* of dying. As a friend said recently, 'It's not
death that worries me; it's dying.'

Ask anyone who has been sick, or has nursed a loved one through
a time of illness, and they will tell you that the long nights are the
worst. When darkness falls outside, it can sometimes affect our
awareness of God's nearness. That is why David speaks in Psalm 30
of weeping 'enduring for a night,' but 'joy' coming 'in the morning'
(v. 5).

This psalm has a parallel in the story of King Hezekiah (Isa. 36-
39) and another psalm which Hezekiah himself composed at the
time of his sickness (Isa. 38:10-20). In fact, some of the thoughts are
almost identical, so much so that some have suggested Hezekiah
knew Psalm 30 well. Through the centuries, great men in times of
crisis have found help in this psalm. We shall use some of King
Hezekiah's words to illustrate what Psalm 30 is trying to tell us.

Believers can be ill

David writes this psalm to thank God for granting recovery from sickness. 'You have healed me,' he cries (v. 2). In the opening verse he uses a word that elsewhere means to lift a bucket out of a well. This is what he says: 'You have lifted me up, and have not let my foes rejoice over me.' It is as though he had fallen into a well and God had placed a rope around him and lifted him out! He continues the imagery in verse 3: 'You have kept me alive, that I should not go down to the pit.' The word 'pit' can also be translated 'well'.

What does it mean to be cast into a well? One of the things the psalmist mentions is his inability to 'see God's face' (v.7).

Most of us have pictures of loved ones around the house. We look at them, at their faces, and sometimes we engage in imaginary conversations with them. It encourages us, and our hearts are warmed. Our relationship with God is something like that. When we have come to know him in his Son we feel that as his adopted children we are allowed to look him in the face (cf. Ps. 27:8-9; 31:16; 67:1). How awful it is when a barrier comes down and we feel estranged from him again! Sickness sometimes does that, as David testifies here. Pain had hidden God's face: in reality he was still there, but David could not see him any more.

Maybe you have felt like that. In that case this psalm has something to say to you.

Healing is a subject fraught with difficulty and discussions about it have to face emotive responses from sincere folk who are longing for release from pain, either for themselves or someone they love. Dismissive statements of the order, 'God does not miraculously heal today,' are less than helpful. We are encouraged to take all our burdens to Jesus, and disease is the greatest burden some Christians know. This is where 'Doctor Jesus' offers us so much help.

Caution is what we need at this point. After all, wild and extravagant claims are made these days. Anyone even hinting at the possibility of the eradication of disease is not reading the Bible properly. The entire world is under a curse and out of joint. Christians are part of this world and in no way exempt from sin's consequences. If Christians can claim freedom from ill-health as a benefit of faith, as some seem to be saying, does that mean that they are never going to die? Death is, after all, the end-result of the process of illness and decay. An argument that takes us down this road is muddled and confused.

What is more, such disputants must reckon with Bible facts: that Jesus himself did not make healing a priority in his ministry; that there were times when he deliberately abandoned crowds who had come to witness his healing powers (Mark 3:7-12); that Paul did not claim healing for his companion Timothy (1 Tim. 5:23); that Trophimus was left sick at Miletus, something which is not described as a failure on the apostle's part (2 Tim. 4:20); that Epaphroditus nearly died from his sickness (Phil. 2:25-27); and Paul was no stranger to pain (2 Cor. 12:7-9).

In the apostle's own case, a threefold intensive session of prayer to the Divine Healer did not remove the offending irritation. A failure of faith? Hardly! It was just another case whereby the Lord taught the lesson that a reminder of our mortality will wean us from undue love for the things of this world and keep our focus fixed on his Son and the glory that awaits his children.

All of us have known illness in one form or another. Most of us have been laid aside with the flu or a migraine or a broken leg. Some have known far more serious and life-threatening illnesses. At such times we have cried to the Lord for healing and he has granted it. What a wonderful thing that is, and how we have wanted to thank God for his mercies to us at such times! That was David's experience in this psalm. Hezekiah, too, had known something similar.

Hezekiah was a good king. There had been no king like him, apart from David and Solomon (2 Kings 18:5). Chronicles says of him, 'And in every work that he began in the service of the house of God, in the law and in the commandment, to seek his God, he did it with all his heart. So he prospered'(2 Chr. 31:21). Yet, despite his godliness, Hezekiah became ill.

We could understand it of a man like Uzziah. He had presumed to go into the temple and offer incense, something which only the priests could do. He had broken God's way of doing things. The leprosy which he contracted is understandable. But why did Hezekiah fall ill?

Hezekiah's story

Like David, Hezekiah was a man who loved working for God. He was a man of great faith and prayer. He often consulted with the prophet Isaiah. He wanted to be sure that he was doing God's will.

His concern, as Solomon's before him, was that God's people worship him in the appointed way (2 Chr. 29:35; cf. 8:16). His predecessor, Ahaz, had closed the temple doors. Hezekiah had reopened them on 'the first day of the first month' of his reign. The very first thing he did was to bring Judah back to God. He knew that men's lives cannot be changed unless first their hearts are turned towards God.

Reformation took place, including the reintroduction of the Passover, long since neglected (2 Chr. 30:26). Israel to the north had been overrun (in 722 BC) by the powerful Assyrian army, which was now threatening Judah itself. Over 27,000 captives had been taken when Samaria fell to the Assyrians, and its overthrow was to terminate the existence of the northern kingdom of Israel as an independent state. As the Assyrian forces marched southwards, capturing such prize cities as Lachish, thirty miles south-west of Jerusalem, Hezekiah could do nothing but retreat into the city. It became both a fortress and a prison. Sennacherib sent as his representative Rabshakeh, one his most senior officials, to demand the unconditional surrender of Jerusalem (2 Kings 18:19-25). Sennacherib boasted that Hezekiah was imprisoned 'like a bird in a cage in Jerusalem, his royal city'. The siege of Jerusalem was to last for over three years.

Hezekiah's most adventurous work was the construction of the Siloam tunnel. Jerusalem's only source of water came from two springs, both of which lay outside the city gates. One, the spring of Gihon, was situated in the Kidron Valley. Hezekiah's engineers blocked up the entrance to these springs, thus denying the Assyrian invaders any access to the water. At the same time they built an underground tunnel bringing fresh supplies of water into the city (2 Kings 20:20; cf. 2 Chr. 32:4, 30. The tunnel was rediscovered in 1880). Isaiah, too, comments on this project (Isa. 22:8-11).

This was to be the practical way in which God kept his people during these years. Then, one night, in answer to Hezekiah's prayers, 186,000 Assyrian soldiers were slain by 'the angel of God'. Sennacherib was sent home with a 'flea in his ear'. Hezekiah's prayers had been answered; God had saved Jerusalem.

Thus Hezekiah was a good man. Not that he did everything right: occasionally he showed his lack of faith by discussing treaties with Egypt and as a result received strong criticism from Isaiah (Isa. 30:1-3). But on the whole, Hezekiah followed the will of God for his life. And yet, he became ill.[2]

David's case is a little different, but he, like Hezekiah, became ill.

Illness strikes

It's the kind of news we all dread to hear: someone we love has cancer. No matter how many advances have been made to soften the blow, it still sends a shiver through most people.

Hezekiah was in his mid-thirties when he was told that his illness was terminal. Doctors can be wrong, but this word came from God! Everything seemed so utterly hopeless.

Suffering is a great puzzle. The book of Job is devoted to this problem. Here was another good and upright man, yet he was to lose his children, property and health all within a few days (Job 1; 2). Some of his counsellors thought Job was at fault; he must have sinned in some way to deserve this kind of treatment (Job 8:20). There are those who feel a calling to tell others in pain that they must have sinned or else they would not be suffering. This is the counsel of the heartless and cruel. Sickness and sin are sometimes connected (1 Cor.11:30), but it is not nearly as simple as that.

Today we are living at a time when a 'healing epidemic' exists. Books by the score arrive at my desk cheerfully announcing that Christians have nothing to fear from sickness, as long as they live close to God. It is not God's will for those whose lives are really consecrated to be anything but successful. Jesus came to make us whole, and that means healthy! One writer confidently asserts, 'The Israelites were never sick.' And this despite the fact that not only David and Hezekiah, but Jacob, Elisha and Daniel were all ill at some time (see Gen. 48; 2 Kings 14; Dan. 7).Only in heaven shall we be free from the effects of sickness.

Don't let me die!

No one wants to die! Or do they? When life has grown difficult some people prefer to die. Solomon pictures life 'under the sun' (i. e. without God) and says of it, 'Therefore I praised the dead who were already dead, more than the living who are still alive' (Eccles. 4:2). There are times when life is so unfair that we wish we were dead.

Psalm 30 also expresses this thought. David could see no profit in dying:

> 'What profit is there in my blood,
> When I go down to the pit?
> Will the dust praise you?
> Will it declare your truth?'

                                                                    (v.9).

These are quite extraordinary words. This is not the way Christians face up to death — or is it?

Hezekiah had no great longing to die, either. This is how he puts it:

> 'I said,
> "In the prime of my life
> I shall go to the gates of Sheol;
> I am deprived of the remainder of my years."
> I said,
> "I shall not see YAH,
> The Lord in the land of the living;
> I shall observe man no more among the inhabitants of the
>   world.
> My life span is gone,
> Taken from me like a shepherd's tent;
> I have cut off my life like a weaver.
> He cuts me off from the loom;
> From day until night you make an end of me.
> I have considered until morning —
> Like a lion,
> So he breaks all my bones;
> From day until night you make an end of me.
> Like a crane or a swallow, so I chattered;
> I mourned like a dove;
> My eyes fail from looking upward.
> O Lord, I am oppressed;
> Undertake for me!
>
> "What shall I say?
> He has both spoken to me,

And he himself has done it.
I shall walk carefully all my years
In the bitterness of my soul.
O Lord, by these things men live;
And in all these things is the life of my spirit;
So you will restore me and make me live.
Indeed it was for my own peace
That I had great bitterness;
But you have lovingly delivered my soul from the pit of
    corruption,
For you have cast all my sins behind your back.
For Sheol cannot thank you,
Death cannot praise you;
Those who go down to the pit cannot hope for your truth.
The living, the living man, he shall praise you,
As I do this day;
The father shall make known your truth to the children.

"The Lord was ready to save me;
Therefore we will sing my songs with stringed
    instruments
All the days of our life in the house of the Lord'"

(Isa. 38:10-20).

It must be terrible to feel like this: as though one's life was being dismantled like a shepherd's tent, which had just been pitched the night before! No wonder his cries resemble the mournful cooing of certain birds. He did not want to die. Hezekiah was young and he had no heir. In the grave his voice would be silent. That was why David likened death to being in a pit. This is not a denial of the truth that at death the believer's soul goes immediately into the presence of Christ. Not at all. But we must appreciate how slowly this truth emerges in the unfolding revelation of God's Word. Death, thinking merely in terms of the physical life, is a terrible condition. The realm of the physically dead (Sheol) is said to have bars (Job 17:16), to be a dark and gloomy place (Job 17:13), and to be a monster with an insatiable appetite (Prov. 27:20; 30:15-16; Isa. 5:14; Hab. 2:5). But, even in the Old Testament, the believer expected life to continue after death, as the following passage makes clear: 'For you will not leave my soul in Sheol, nor will you allow your Holy One to see

corruption' (Ps. 16:10). This passage from the psalms is cited by
Peter in his Pentecost sermon and seen as a prophecy of Jesus' own
resurrection. David must also have believed it about himself.

Healing

God healed David (v.2). He also restored Hezekiah. In the case of
the latter, Isaiah was sent with these words: 'I have heard your
prayer, I have seen your tears; and I will add to your days fifteen
years' (Isa. 38:5). As a sign of God's healing work Hezekiah was
granted a sign of God's power: the shadow of the obelisk sundial on
the steps of Jerusalem went back by ten degrees (indicating that the
time had gone back by five hours).

It is important to understand that God does not always heal in
answer to prayer. There is nothing peculiar about this. It is not just
in healing that prayer is not answered. Unanswered prayer should
not overburden us. It is meant to teach us the lesson that God knows
better than we do; that there are some things it is better for us not to
receive, at least, not yet! We are not the best judges of what is good
for us! Paul felt confident that he would be more useful for God
without the 'thorn in the flesh'. He was wrong! And his threefold cry
for its removal, undoubtedly prayed in faith, only served to underline the fact that, despite his privileged position as an apostle,
there was one who knew better than he what was best for him.

God healed David and Hezekiah and both responded with praise
(Ps. 30:4; Isa. 38:20).

God healed John Wesley, too. Travelling by horseback and
preaching out of doors soon took their toll on Wesley's health. At the
end of October 1753 he fell ill with a fever. After attempts to relieve
the pain by using cinchona bark (quinine) he fell into a worse
condition. George Whitefield, who paid him a visit, was greatly
distressed by his condition. His physician, John Fothergill, diag-
nosed 'galloping consumption' (advanced tuberculosis). He offered
little hope. A wealthy banker, Ebenezer Blackwell, took the
Wesleys to a grand country residence, 'The Limes'. John Wesley
loved it there, even though he expected to die shortly. In fact, he
drafted an inscription for his tombstone:

Here lieth
The body of JOHN WESLEY

A brand plucked from the burning,
Who died of Consumption in the fifty-first year of his
    age
And leaving, after his debts are paid, ten pounds
    behind him;
Praying,
God be merciful to me, an unprofitable servant.

His brother Charles came down to see him, weeping when he saw his condition. Charles rode back and summoned the Foundry (the Wesleys' home congregation in London) to urgent prayer, requesting Whitefield to do the same. 'If prayers could detain the heavenly chariots,' commented Whitefield, 'Wesley should not leave us yet. But if the decree is gone forth that you must now fall asleep in Jesus, may he kiss your soul away, and give you to die in the embraces of triumphant love! If in the land of the living, I hope to pay my respects to you next week. If not, rev. and very dear sire, F-A-R-E-W-E-L-L.' Adding, 'My heart is too big, tears trickle down too fast, and you, I fear, too weak for me to enlarge. Underneath you may there be Christ's everlasting arms. I commend you to his never-failing mercy, and am, rev. and very dear sir, your most affectionate, sympathising, and afflicted younger brother in the gospel of our common Lord, G.W.'

By the time this letter had reached Lewisham, Wesley was riding again. A month or so later he was busy writing and preparing for the next battle in the emerging Methodist Church.[3]

When such deliverances come, especially in answer to protracted prayer, there is only one fitting response: gratitude! Little wonder the psalmist begins and ends the psalm with thanksgiving: 'I will extol you, O Lord ... I will give thanks to you for ever' (vv.1, 12).

Psalm 119, part 2

'How can a young man cleanse his way?
By taking heed according to your word.
With my whole heart I have sought you;
Oh, let me not wander from your commandments!
Your word I have hidden in my heart,
That I might not sin against you.
Blessed are you, O Lord!
Teach me your statutes.
With my lips I have declared
All the judgements of your mouth.
I have rejoiced in the way of your testimonies,
As much as in all riches.
I will meditate on your precepts,
And contemplate your ways.
I will delight myself in your statutes;
I will not forget your word'

(vv. 9-16).

5.
Progress in holiness

Psalm 119, part 2

We have already seen that a key idea in Psalm 119 is the need for holiness. Its opening verse underlines it: 'Blessed are the undefiled in the way, who walk in the law of the Lord!' Section 2 of the psalm (vv.9-16) brings it into sharper focus by highlighting both the hindrances and the helps to holiness.

Hindrances to holiness

Likeness to Jesus Christ, which is what holiness is all about, is a process that is constantly under attack. Two factors hinder our progress: indwelling sin and the law.

The problem of indwelling sin

'With my whole heart I have sought you;
Oh, let me not wander from your commandments!
Your word have I hidden in my heart,
That I might not sin against you'

(vv.10-11).

The psalmist is troubled by his sin. Believers are always troubled by sin. Sin is an enemy to be destroyed.

As we have already seen, the psalmist has already stated that the overall dominion of sin has been broken: 'They also do no iniquity; they walk in his ways' (v. 3). But sin remains as a powerful influence in a believer's life. It is interesting that Paul describes the power of indwelling sin as itself being a law: 'I find then a law, that evil is

present with me...' (Rom. 7:21). Its effect is twofold: to draw away
the heart from its affection for God (vv. 10-11), and to weaken the
mind in its practice of spiritual meditation (vv. 15, 23, 97).

Indwelling sin is a powerful force. John Owen once described its
power in this way: imagine a horse having lost its rider. Its dominating power is destroyed. But 'Like an untamed horse, which having
first cast off its rider, [it] runs away with fierceness and rage.'[1]

The presence of indwelling sin is bad enough, but the law adds
to the problem by highlighting it.

The problem of the law

We usually read verse 9 as a question and answer: 'How can a young
man cleanse his way?' (Answer) 'By taking heed according to your
word.' But what if, instead, we read it like this: 'How can a young
man cleanse his way by taking heed according to your word?' The
difference lies in where we place the question mark. Reading it the
second way implies that the psalmist is finding God's law itself a
problem to holiness. God's law is not so much the answer to the
problem of holiness as an added difficulty.[2]

To read the verse this way may seem strange at first, especially
since the psalmist spends most of his time telling us how wonderful
God's law is. How can he rejoice in God's law and at the same time
find it an obstacle to serving God? Paul, too, has a similar problem.
The 'law ... is good,' he insists (Rom. 7:16). Yet in the very same
chapter he tells us that the law is an obstacle to holiness. This is the
burden of Romans 7:14-25.

The law is God's way of showing us that we are sinners. Rules
and regulations unkept and broken show us up in a bad light. Worse,
the law actually goads sin into active rebellion. 'But sin, taking
opportunity by the commandment, produced in me all manner of
evil desire. For apart from the law sin was dead' (Rom. 7:8).

The word Paul uses (*aphorme*, translated 'opportunity') means
that from which an attack is launched. It is used for a base of
operations, a spring-board for attack. The law is the enemy's
control-room where schemes are drawn up to destroy us. Who, for
example, hasn't seen a sign written on a door: 'Private: Keep Out',
and has not immediately wanted to see what was on the other side?

Worse still, the law is powerless to help us to do the good it itself
prescribes: 'I was alive once without the law, but when the

commandment came, sin revived and I died. And the commandment, which was to bring life, I found to bring death' (Rom. 7:9-10).

Paul may well be describing his own personal experience here. As a young boy, ignorant of much of the law, he was alive; but as soon as he became aware of the law's demands (perhaps at the age of thirteen when Jewish boys became 'sons of the commandment') he came under the judgement of the law and, spiritually, he died. Spiritual death is what the law highlights.

Apart from the law, the apostle Paul tells us in an autobiographical statement, he would have had no knowledge of sin (Rom. 7:7). The law, at least in one of its aspects, shows us up badly. The Scottish preacher Alexander Whyte once described the law as 'the dark lines in the Almighty's face'. The law, he seemed to say, was God frowning at us. No wonder the psalmist is burdened by sin. The law only exacerbates his condition, making it worse minute by minute. Even as a believer, the law points up the corruption of his heart, making him cry out, 'O wretched man that I am!' (Rom. 7:24).

The law shows us three things: what God is like, what God expects and our sinfulness. We need only a brief acquaintance with God's law to appreciate that the law cannot save us. We can *never* keep it and the law points this out to us again and again. John Owen once described the way the law points up the nature of our sinfulness by comparing it to a 'poor beast that hath a deadly arrow sticking in its sides, that makes it restless wherever it is and whatever it doth'.[3]

Someone may well be asking the question: if God's law cannot save us (which it cannot) why then did God give the law? Part of the answer is that the law makes us appreciate the infinite value of Jesus Christ! He is the only one who has ever fully obeyed the law. The law shows us the futility of trying to earn salvation by obedience to God's law and instead shows us that salvation is by grace, through faith in Jesus Christ.

A debtor to mercy alone,
Of covenant mercy I sing;
Nor fear, with thy righteousness on,
My person and offering to bring.
The terrors of law and of God
With me can have nothing to do;

My Saviour's obedience and blood
Hide all my transgressions from view.

(Augustus Toplady).

Helps to holiness

The psalm also has some positive things to say to us. It provides
us with helps for holiness. There are three of them.

1. We should meditate upon God's Word

Psalm 119 is not only about meditation; it is meditation. Martin
Luther once wrote, 'It often happens that I lose myself in such rich
thoughts [literally, 'that my thoughts go for a walk'] in one petition
of the Lord's Prayer and then I let all other six petitions go. When
such rich good thoughts come, one should let the other prayers go
and give room to these thoughts, listen to them in silence and by no
means suppress them. For here the Holy Spirit himself is preaching
and one word of his sermon is better than thousands of our own
prayers. Therefore I have often learned more in one prayer than I
could have obtained from much reading and thinking.'[4]

In Psalm 119 the writer is concerned to point out to us the value
of using our minds: 'Teach me your statutes' (v. 12), he writes. He
uses the word 'understanding' five times (vv. 34, 73, 125, 144, 169).
He wants to know the full range of God's demands and respond
appropriately: 'Give me understanding and I shall keep your law'
(v.34). 'I will meditate on your precepts' (v.15).

The Bible is a book to meditate upon. Meditation is a spiritual
duty which brings spiritual life and a sense of well-being (Rom. 8:6).
We should let our minds 'go for a leisurely walk' as we read the
Bible. This psalm in particular is designed for meditation; its
magnificent scenery is to be relished. And it takes time! Psalm 119
encourages us to throw away books on 'How to speed-read'!

The key to understanding this psalm is to enter into its own
thought world. In the East they practise 'lotus meditation', whereby
every thought must eventually return to the main central thought (in
the way that the petals of a lotus flower all focus on a central stem).
The central thought here, of course, is the value of God's law. His
law is wonderful. Time and time again, the psalmist returns to this
thought.

All Scripture is meant to be read this way. As we read the Bible a two-way dialogue takes place: we interrogate Scripture and Scripture interrogates us. That can be quite unnerving on occasions. Those who read their Bibles humbly and submissively can expect blessing and encouragement. Letting our minds 'walk through the Bible' will help us appreciate more of the one who wrote it. Interrogating the Bible's words, and allowing these words to interrogate us, brings a realization that we are talking to God himself, and this will aid our growth in holiness.

A test of our spiritual-mindedness is the way thoughts arise within our mind, says John Owen.[5] A Christian's spiritual thoughts are like children living in their parents' house. From time to time guests may come and go. They do not live there. Their presence is only for a season. So those who are not Christians may have an occasional spiritual thought. But 'Children are owned in the house, are missed if they are out of the way, and have their daily provision constantly made for them. So it is with these occasional thoughts about spiritual things.'[6]

2. *We ought to seek the Lord with all our hearts*

'With my whole heart I have sought you; oh, let me not wander from your commandments!' (v. 10). Clearly, the psalmist is aware that sin draws away the heart from its affection for God.

The Old Testament regarded the heart as the centre of the whole man — physical, intellectual and psychological. When Jeremiah wished to express how deep-rooted sin lay in man, he put it in terms of the heart: 'The heart is deceitful above all things, and desperately wicked' (Jer.17:9). The word he uses (translated 'deceitful') means 'slippery'. 'He's a slippery customer,' a friend of mine sometimes says of someone he mistrusts. This is an accurate description of our hearts: slippery, prone to be unfaithful. It is also the testimony of a well-known hymn:

Oh, to grace how great a debtor
Daily I'm constrained to be;
Let that grace now, like a fetter,
Bind my wandering heart to thee.
Prone to wander, Lord, I feel it,

Prone to leave the God I love;
Here's my heart, oh, take and seal it,
Seal it for thy courts above.

(Robert Robinson).

Seeking God with all of our hearts brings into sharper focus the grace and power of God to overcome sin in our lives.

3. *We are to rejoice in his truth*

'With my lips I have declared
All the judgements of your mouth.
I have rejoiced in the way of your testimonies,
As much as in all riches'

(vv.13-14).

When did reading the Bible last produce in you a sense of overwhelming joy? It should! Why not take up your Bible right now and prove it for yourself?

Psalm 54

'Save me, O God, by your name,
And vindicate me by your strength.
Hear my prayer, O God;
Give ear to the words of my mouth.
For strangers have risen up against me,
And oppressors have sought after my life;
They have not set God before them.

Behold, God is my helper;
The Lord is with those who uphold my life.
He will repay my enemies for their evil.
Cut them off in your truth.

I will freely sacrifice to you;
I will praise your name, O Lord, for it is good.
For he has delivered me out of all trouble;
And my eye has seen its desire upon my enemies.'

6.
Spiritual recovery after a fall

Psalm 54

When you fall flat on your face, there is at least the consolation that you cannot fall any further. There is only one thing left to do: attempt to get up again. Psalm 54 (like Psalms 30 and 56) is one of fourteen psalms carrying headings which identify them with specific historical events in David's life.[1]

David had fallen. Saul's incessant campaign had got to him, and David was rattled. He had done what most of us do under pressure: he took it out on his best friend. 'What have I done?' David protested to Jonathan (1 Sam. 20:1). It wasn't fair! Why should he be treated like this? Had not Samuel promised that he should be the next King of Israel? Why then was his life in constant danger?

Jonathan was Saul's son and David even went as far as to suggest that his friend might be in league with his megalomaniac father! 'Kill me yourself,' David had said to Jonathan, 'why should you bring me to your father?' (1 Sam. 20:8).

We have all known what it is to feel like this. Life can sometimes seem so unfair. The way we cope with irritation is a test of the reality of our relationship with God. David decided that God's promises were fine, so long as things were going well. But in times of danger, he thought he needed to take things into his own hands. The best way to emerge victorious in this situation was to lie.

So it was that David and Jonathan schemed, devising an elaborate story that David was needed at home in Bethlehem and that the invitation to Saul's special three-day festival to mark the New Moon would have to be declined. If Saul should be annoyed, Jonathan would come to a predetermined spot for archery practice with a young lad and by a system of signals David, who would be hiding nearby, would know it was time to leave. It all sounds a bit like playing at boy scouts except that for David it meant the beginning of a downward spiral of lies and deceit.

Fleeing from Saul, David arrived at Nob, the 'city of the priests', where he continued his fanciful tales. This time he insisted that he was engaged on a 'top-secret mission', convincing Ahimelech the priest to part with the Bread of the Presence, something which only the priests were allowed to eat (1 Sam. 21:1-9). The unwitting complicity of Ahimelech would later cost him his life, together with eighty-five other men 'who wore a linen ephod'. Saul, in a murderous rage, persuaded Doeg the Edomite to kill them (1 Sam. 22). Our sins affect others, and nowhere is this seen to more deadly effect than in this incident.

From Nob, David fled to Gath, a Philistine stronghold. What possessed David to go there is anybody's guess. He probably thought that he could become an anonymous mercenary in the Philistine army. It was never going to work. He was recognized immediately as the one who had killed their most famous soldier, Goliath. After all, David had Goliath's sword with him (1 Sam. 22:10).

David was reduced to feigning madness to save his skin, dribbling from his mouth and scribbling graffiti on the city walls until the Philistines (who were superstitious about mental illness) persuaded him to leave.

From Gath, David wandered, first to the cave of Adullam, where he gathered together a ramshackle army of about four hundred men (1 Sam. 22:1-2); then to Mispah in Moab, where he left his family for safe keeping from Saul (1 Sam. 22:3); then on to the forest of Hereth (NIV has 'Horesh'), where David and his men rescued the city of Keilah, which was being plundered by the Philistines (1 Sam. 23:1-13). From here, David moved to the mountains, in the Wilderness of Ziph, where 'Saul sought him every day, but God did not deliver him into his hand' (1 Sam. 23:14).

The Wilderness of Ziph was wild and inhospitable country, to the south and east of Hebron. It was a safe place to hide, except, that is, from those who knew the terrain best — the Ziphites. The Ziphites, like the inhabitants of Keilah, belonged to the tribe of Judah (as did David). But they were loyal to Saul and betrayed David's whereabouts to him. David's assessment of them was that they were 'strangers' and 'oppressors' who 'have not set God before them' (Ps. 54:3).

Psalm 54 was written at a time of deep disappointment in David's life. It was one thing to be hunted by a megalomaniac like Saul. It was quite another to be betrayed by people from your own tribe. Betrayal is always a difficult thing to handle. What happened to David is a picture of what happened to Christ. He too was betrayed by his own people.

This was one of the lowest points in David's life. He had followed the sinful inclinations of his heart. He had responded to irritation with lies and deceit and he had paid dearly for it. Any chance of reconciliation with Saul was over; the blood of Ahimelech and eighty-five priests was on his hands; he had raised the suspicions of fellow Israelites by attempting to become a mercenary in the army of the Philistine Achish. Now, he had been betrayed by his own tribesmen, the Ziphites. He had really reached rock-bottom. However, low points are also opportunities for repentance, and this is what we see in this psalm.

Psalm 54 is a psalm about spiritual recovery. It is a psalm of maturity. Three features of this psalm highlight the way of David's spiritual recovery.

1. A renewed prayer life

'Hear my prayer, O God; give ear to the words of my mouth,' David cries (v. 2). It is not extraordinary to find David praying in the psalms. The psalms are, after all, the covenant song-book of the Bible, expressing the deepest spiritual conversations of God's people with God.

What is extraordinary is the context in which the psalm was written. David is contemplating the treachery of his fellow Judeans. He has just emerged from a battle with the Philistines at Keilah and it was there that we read that David 'enquired of the Lord' as to what he should do (1 Sam. 23:2,4,10,12). Nowhere in the preceding three chapters do we find David asking the Lord for anything. The entire story of his wanderings from Naioth to Nob to Gath to Adullam's cave is free from any reference to the will of God. Only now that David has experienced the bitterness of a lifestyle which betrays more of the world than of one who knows God is he once more asking God for advice.

Asking the Lord for guidance was the theme of Psalm 25. Being careful in the matter of God's will is a sign of growing maturity.

This is what Paul desired for every Christian: 'I beseech you therefore, brethren, by the mercies of God, that you present your bodies a living sacrifice, holy, acceptable to God, which is your reasonable service. And do not be conformed to this world, but be transformed by the renewing of your mind, that you may prove what is that good and acceptable and perfect will of God' (Rom. 12:1-2).

Doing God's will is the most important thing in our lives. And here, as he does so often, David reflects something of the coming Saviour. For it was Jesus' own testimony that he came to do the will of his Father (John 5:30; cf. Luke 22:42). The ministry of David's greater Son is foreshadowed in the life of David, and this is especially so in his trials and sufferings as the Lord's anointed.

The shadow of death that lay across the valley of the Wilderness of Ziph is paralleled in the ministry of Christ. We only have to remember the agonies of Christ in the Garden of Gethsemane to recall just how similar an experience David had himself felt. Jesus, of course, suffered immeasurably more than David ever did. When Jesus contemplated the horror of betrayal and the sufferings that would result as a consequence, his perspiration was like drops of blood falling to the ground. Yet, throughout the struggle he was resolute: 'Not my will, but yours, be done!' And in the crucible of his affliction, as David contemplates death at the hand of Saul, he mirrors his Lord.

Ask the question of your own life: 'What is my prayer life like at the moment?' Prayerlessness is one of those symptoms of decay in our spiritual lives, in much the same way that a cold east wind is often a sign of the onset of winter. Samuel Rutherford, who had sustained the loss of his wife and two children, lived in times of persecution. Charles I wished to reinstate episcopacy in Scotland and had Rutherford tried and imprisoned in Aberdeen. Referring often to his cell as 'Christ's palace', he wrote to a friend, Lady Culross, asking for prayer that in his trial he might have strength to praise God. 'I see,' he remarked in the letter, 'grace grows best in winter.'[2]

Like Rutherford, David found that a winter in his spiritual experience was also an opportunity for God to work. What about you? Is your life marked out by this kind of determination to do God's will whatever the cost? Praying for God's will is a growth experience.

2. A renewed trust in God

The key to understanding David's growth and maturity lies in his growing awareness of just how much he could trust God with his life. Talking about spiritual matters is one thing; proving them is another. 'Behold,' David says, 'God is my helper; the Lord is with those who uphold my life' (v. 4).

The second part of this verse has caused one or two problems. How can God be among those who have helped David? Thus, some translations have rendered it differently, including the New International Version, which has 'The Lord is the one who sustains me.' But there is no real problem here. David is only seeing God's hand in the human side of his life. David had some 600 men with him, protecting him, but they were God's instruments. Whatever powers they had were only given as a result of God's provision. Trusting God, to work either directly or through our friends, is what David means here. He had come to prove that, despite even his own waywardness and stupidity, there was a greater power at work in his life.

Even in Gath, when he had placed himself unnecessarily among his enemies, David experienced God's protection. He was to write about it in Psalm 56:1-3:

'Be merciful to me, O God, for man would swallow me
    up;
Fighting all day he oppresses me.
My enemies would hound me all day,
For there are many who fight against me, O Most High.

Whenever I am afraid, I will trust in you.
In God (I will praise his word),
In God I have put my trust;
I will not fear.
What can flesh do to me?'

As Christians, living in our Father's world, we can have this confidence too. We become afraid of all sorts of things, but our Father will not let anything come into our lives that will take away from us our relationship with him. There may be difficulties, of course, but these things are to teach us to rely on him rather than on ourselves (2 Cor. 1:9).

3. A renewed love for our enemies

David's response to the ungrateful Ziphites is mentioned twice in
the psalm. In verse 5, he asserts that God 'will repay my enemies for
their evil'. At the end of the psalm, he recalls that 'My eye has seen
its desire upon my enemies' (v.7). We have already seen this kind
of response from David before in Psalm 5. There he had said,

> 'Pronounce them guilty, O God!
> Let them fall by their own counsels;
> Cast them out in the multitude of their transgressions,
> For they have rebelled against you'

(v.10).

I did not comment on this verse at the time, but perhaps now is
the place to do so. These responses in the psalms, sometimes
referred to as imprecations, have occasioned much concern among
serious readers of the Bible. In view of Jesus' instructions to turn the
other cheek, to pray for one's enemies (Matt. 5:39,44), and especially his own example on the cross (see Luke 23:34), these
responses in the psalms seem out of place. Some, C. S. Lewis for
example, have seen these verses as the outpouring of hatred, the
reaction of a sinful heart to wrongdoing.[3] That David was capable
of revenge is beyond question. We see this, for example, in 1
Samuel 25, where David is filled with revenge against Nabal for
refusing to give him and his men any food. Had it not been for the
intervention of Nabal's wife, Abigail, David would no doubt have
slaughtered Nabal and his family.

If these outpourings are expressions of hatred and anger, does
this not pose some difficult questions about the inspiration of the
psalms? In fact, what needs to be seen immediately is the fact that
in every instance in the psalms where such remarks are found, they
are not expressions of desire for personal revenge, but rather a
desire that God be *just* in the way he deals with those who are, and
remain, his enemies. David wants no more than would be the case
if the situation were being dealt with in a civil court (see Deut. 25:1-
3). David at no time sought any personal revenge on the Ziphites.
Nor, for that matter, did he ever attempt to get his own back on Saul,
even when providence provided a breathtaking opportunity.

Saul, seeking to relieve himself in the Desert of En Gedi, went inside a cave without realizing that David was only a few feet behind him in the darkness! (1 Sam. 24:1-4). David's men saw this as an opportunity to have done with Saul once and for all. It even looked as though God had arranged for it this way. But David would have none of it. David crept up to Saul and cut off the corner of his robe that he had set aside, but he would not touch Saul himself. Even this action troubled David: 'The Lord forbid that I should do this thing to my master, the Lord's anointed, to stretch out my hand against him, seeing he is the anointed of the Lord' (1 Sam. 24:6).

Later he demonstrated the same concern for the life of his enemy when he, and one of his officers, Abishai, went to Saul's camp at night and while the king was sleeping, took away the water jug and spear that lay near the king's head (1 Sam. 26).

Showing love to your enemy is a mark of spiritual maturity. David knew enough of the Old Testament to know that God expects his children to love their neighbour (Lev. 19:18). By Jesus' day, however, like so many other Bible principles, this one had been distorted to mean that the opposite was also to be true. If we are to love our neighbour, it follows that we are to hate our enemies, some argued. Jesus reverses the sin-bred instincts of our hearts to retaliate when we are wronged. If someone strikes you on the cheek, turn the other to him as well, he said. If someone wants to sue you and take your tunic, give him your cloak as well, he said. If someone asks you to go a mile with him — a Roman soldier, for example, as a hated representative of an occupying force, could enforce anyone to carry a heavy burden for him — go with him two miles, Jesus says. David reflects that kind of love for his enemies, too, and in so doing he pictures the coming Saviour whose love for his enemies took him to the cross.

It may be that you are wrestling with the problem of wanting to retaliate because someone has done you wrong. Take this psalm and see if it does not help you overcome that feeling!

Psalm 56

'Be merciful to me, O God, for man would swallow me up;
Fighting all day he oppresses me.
My enemies would hound me all day,
For there are many who fight against me, O Most High.

Whenever I am afraid,
I will trust in you.
In God (I will praise his word),
In God I have put my trust;
I will not fear
What can flesh do to me?

All day they twist my words;
All their thoughts are against me for evil.
They gather together,
They hide, they mark my steps,
When they lie in wait for my life.
Shall they escape by iniquity?
In anger cast down the peoples, O God!

You number my wanderings;
Put my tears into your bottle;
Are they not in your book?
When I cry out to you,
Then my enemies will turn back;
This I know, because God is for me.
In God (I will praise his word),
In the Lord (I will praise his word),
In God I have put my trust;
I will not be afraid.
What can man do to me?

Vows made to you are binding upon me, O God;
I will render praises to you,
For you have delivered my soul from death.
Have you not delivered my feet from falling,
That I may walk before God
In the light of the living?'

7.
God's preserving jars

Psalm 56

It's strange what some people keep: old photographs, letters, a wedding dress, a child's first tooth! On my study wall is a photograph taken some thirty years ago of a sheepdog called Floss. She was my best friend at around the age of six!

God keeps things too, so the psalmist tells us. He keeps our tears preserved in a bottle!

'You number my wanderings;
Put my tears into your bottle;
Are they not in your book?'

(Ps. 56:8).[1]

When words fail, tears fall. Mysteriously and wonderfully made as we are, our complicated inner-communication system knows when to signal defeat — and tears come. They are the Creator's built-in safety-valve for pent-up emotions.

Even grown men cry. Jeremiah was nicknamed 'the weeping prophet' for he would often bury his head in his hands and weep for the hardness of Israel (Lam. 1:12-16; 3:46-50; Jer. 50:4). And Jesus wept (John 11:35).

One tear-drop summons the King of heaven. It was this thought that comforted King David in a time of crisis.

A sudden rise to fame

Like Psalm 54, this psalm was written early in David's career when he fled from King Saul to Gath, the Philistine stronghold (1 Sam.

21). Following a secret anointing in Bethlehem by the prophet Samuel, David had entered into Saul's service as court musician. The relationship proved difficult, partly because of Saul's megalomaniac tendencies, and partly because of David's popularity with the people. The latter was due to his native charm: he was young, handsome and brave (1 Sam. 16:18). But it was the slaying of Goliath that changed the course of David's life. For a shepherd boy, armed with a few pebbles and a sling, to overcome and kill a notorious enemy warrior, was more than some people could take in. It brought David into the realm of folklore.

Women sang openly in the streets of his powers: 'Saul has slain his thousands, and David his ten thousands' (1 Sam. 18:7). And Saul bitterly resented it.

From that moment David became a hunted man. As we have already seen, David conspired with Jonathan a web of deceit that compounded lies with folly, and fleeing from Saul he found himself in the Philistine stronghold of Gath.

David had barely begun his life of usefulness in God's service and his world was falling apart. What did David learn in Gath? Let us see if we can summarize some of the lessons from Psalm 56.

1. Learning from our mistakes

We see, firstly, that there is no problem too great for God. Some of David's troubles were of his own making; others were not. Either way, troubles abounded for him and his many enemies were trying to kill him (vv.1-2). Had he not confessed to Jonathan the memorable words, 'There is but a step between me and death'? (1 Sam. 20:3). But David learnt something in Gath that would stand him in good stead for the rest of his life:

'Whenever I am afraid,
I will trust in you.
In God (I will praise his word),
In God I have put my trust;
I will not fear.
What can flesh do to me?'

(vv. 3-4).

In a companion psalm, written at the same time and expressing much the same sentiments, David puts it this way: 'Many are the afflictions of the righteous, but the Lord delivers him out of them all' (Ps. 34:19). How does he do this? 'The angel of the Lord encamps all around those who fear him, and delivers them' (Ps. 34:7).

Perhaps you are tempted to say that your problems are special. No one understands their complexities. There is no one who can offer you sympathy, for you are special; when someone tries to offer a word of encouragement you simply shrug it off by saying, 'But you don't understand! My problem is too big for God!'

Think about that for a minute. I'm sure that every one of us has thought something like that at some time or another. But it makes no sense! If there is some power in the universe that is stronger than God, then God is not God!

I like the way R. C. Sproul writes. He has a way of saying a great deal in one short sentence. One of them goes like this: 'If God is not sovereign, then God is not God.'[2] Once you hear that line you somehow never forget it. And it's true! There isn't a problem that God cannot deal with and solve. That does not mean that the problem is always going to vanish away. You only have to think of Paul's 'thorn in the flesh' to discover that. It is vital for us to recall that sometimes the way he deals with problems is to help us cope with them.

That is what David discovered in Gath. Saul remained David's enemy, and attempts on his life would be made again. But David learnt to trust God more fully than before. The trial had done that.

David, who had known the Lord's help in killing lions and bears and Goliath, discovered that in the darkest time of his life he could trust the Lord with his problems. We need to trust him too if we are to grow in grace and usefulness.

2. Submission

We also find that trials have a way of bringing us into total submission to God. Listen to David in this psalm and you will hear just how much his will has been brought under submission. 'I will trust in you...' (v. 3) 'In God I have put my trust...' (vv. 4, 11). Just how has David come to do this? The companion psalm throws light on it: 'The Lord is near to those who have a broken heart, and saves such as have a contrite spirit' (Ps. 34:18).

God has a way of reducing us to size when we have too high an opinion of ourselves. David's spirit had been broken and brought into submission to God. It was a painful process. It always is. And it was necessary, for unless we are prepared to accept his will for our lives we cannot be useful for him.

The man who would teach us most about 'waiting on God' was himself to learn how difficult a thing it is. Look at his sage advice in Psalm 37:

'Rest in the Lord, and wait patiently for him;
Do not fret because of him who prospers in his way,
Because of the man who brings wicked schemes to pass.'

The sight of evil men and women succeeding in their ways makes us fret. We become anxious. We lose our confidence. We become impatient. We devise schemes to ape them. This is what David did. Now he sees a better way: waiting on God. It was the trial that had taught him this lesson.

Maybe you should ask yourself what area of your life needs to be brought under the lordship of Jesus Christ. The Lord disciplines us to bring us closer to himself. If we are to walk with God in our trials we must learn to 'glory in tribulations' (Rom. 5:3-4).

3. Help is just around the corner

Next we find that in every problem prayer will help us through it. This is how David expresses himself: 'When I cry out to you, then my enemies will turn back' (v. 9). He says the same thing in the companion psalm: 'The eyes of the Lord are on the righteous, and his ears are open to their cry' (Ps. 34:15).

As we have seen, what emerges in this period of David's life that led to Gath is his prayerlessness. He seems to have had more confidence in himself than in God. The deceitfulness that marks out his journey from Gibeah to Gath is directly linked to his low spiritual state.

No believer can live without prayer for long. Sooner or later he discovers that life without communion with the Father is an impoverished one, especially as life gets difficult. E. M. Bounds once wrote, 'Trouble and prayer are closely related to each other. Prayer is of great value to trouble. Trouble often drives men to God in prayer, while prayer is but the voice of men in trouble.'3

No life thrives without much secret communion with God, and these two psalms make up for what is lacking in the story as we find it in 1 Samuel. 'If we are empty and poor,' said the Puritan Thomas Manton, 'it is not because God's hand is straitened, but ours is not opened.'

Tell me, what are you doing with your problems? Maybe, like David, you are taking it out on your best friend. Husbands can bring problems home from the office and dump them on their wives as soon as they enter the front door! Mothers can take out their own frustrations by shouting at their children. But the best way is prayer.

Do what Hezekiah did. When Sennacherib wrote him a letter threatening to destroy Jerusalem he took it immediately into the temple and read it out loud to God, saying, 'O Lord of hosts, God of Israel, the One who dwells between the cherubim, you are God, you alone, of all the kingdoms of the earth. You have made heaven and earth. Incline your ear, O Lord, and hear; open your eyes, O Lord, and see; and hear all the words of Sennacherib, who has sent to reproach the living God. Truly, Lord, the kings of Assyria have laid waste all the nations and their lands, and have cast their gods into the fire; for they were not gods, but the work of men's hands — wood and stone. Therefore they have destroyed them. Now therefore, O Lord our God, save us from his hand, that all the kingdoms of the earth may know that you are the Lord, you alone' (Isa. 37:16-20).

Now that is a real prayer! Your Father in heaven wants you to tell him your worries.

4. He knows

However dark it is, we may be sure that our Father never forgets us. Did you notice that when David makes the point about the Lord preserving his tears in a bottle, he also says that God keeps a diary?

'You number my wanderings;
Put my tears into your bottle;
Are they not in your book?'

(v. 9).

Are you the kind of person who needs to write things down to remember them? I am — and even then I forget! Some folk even write things on their hands! God not only remembers, but he keeps a diary of everything that happens to us.

Why do we think, as we so often do, that when trouble comes it must be because God has forgotten us? What kind of God forgets things? It is altogether an unworthy notion! Just think about it for a minute. Could the Father send his own Son to die in such a terrible way on the cross so that his own children might live, only then to forget all about them? The very idea is unworthy of God.

That God cares, and goes on caring deeply about his children, ought to be self-evident; but Jesus underlines it anyway. Out of some 9,000 species of bird he chose what must be the most common of all to make his point — the sparrow: 'Are not two sparrows sold for a copper coin? And not one of them falls to the ground apart from your Father's will. But the very hairs of your head are all numbered. Do not fear therefore; you are of more value than many sparrows' (Matt. 10:29-31).

I must confess to never having eaten a sparrow (at least not to my knowledge!). Poor folk in Jesus' day might have purchased two for 'a penny' (one sixteenth of a denarius, roughly what a man might earn in day). If the Lord knows all about a sparrow that might drop from the sky, then he most certainly knows and cares about you and me! Next time you see a scruffy sparrow in the garden just remind yourself that God cares for you, no matter what may be happening.

5. God is for me!

We also discover that, whatever happens, nothing can destroy our relationship with God. The hinge on which the entire psalm rotates is the declaration in verse 9: 'God is for me.' Everything follows as a result of this basic confidence that God is on his side. Nor is this psalm alone in ringing the changes on this theme.

The final verses of Romans 8 have been described as the 'Everest' of Christian revelation. Paul is anxious to cheer the hearts of those whom he has wounded in the previous chapter. Having shown that the law speaks only of sin and failure, he is anxious to go on and describe the riches of grace to be found in the gospel. Four gifts of God are underlined as the possession of every Christian:

Acceptance with God (what the Bible sometimes calls right-eousness): 'There is therefore now no condemnation to those who are in Christ Jesus' (Rom. 8:1).

The Holy Spirit: 'But you are not in the flesh but in the Spirit' Rom. 8:9).

Adoption: 'For as many as are led by the Spirit of God, these are the sons of God' (Rom. 8:14).

Security: 'If God is for us, who can be against us?' (Rom. 8:31).

If God is for us, then we are secure. Nothing can be against us. Paul lists all the possibilities and they are all powerless to undo the covenant relationship that exists between a believer and his God.

'If God is for us...' That is precisely what Psalm 56 is reckoning with: the covenant that God makes cannot be undone. Nothing shows us more clearly that God is 'on our side' than the work of Jesus Christ on the cross. Once a person has been made right with God nothing can then undo it — nothing!

What about trouble? Or a handicapped child? Or bankruptcy? Or bereavement? Or ...? Nothing! Nothing! *Nothing!*

6. 'Oh for a heart to praise my God ...'

Finally, we see from this psalm that a praising heart will see us through difficulties. It's easily said (and written about!) but a great deal more difficult in practice. It is much easier to get depressed, or moody, or irritable in difficult times. We make excuses for ourselves all the time when life is hard. I deserve to lose my temper; after all, it has been a difficult day. It is acceptable if I shout at the children; after all, nothing has gone right for me today! Who hasn't reasoned like this at some time or another? But responses of this kind are never right. That is not the way of Psalm 56!

Twice David alludes to his trust in God's Word (vv. 4,10). 'How prone we are,' wrote Calvin, 'to fret and to murmur when it has not pleased God immediately to grant us our requests! Our discontent may not be openly expressed, but it is inwardly felt, when we are left in this manner to depend upon his naked promises.'[4] How true!

What word is David alluding to in these verses? He is not thinking of one particular text, but the covenantal way God deals with his people. The whole Bible is given to us in terms of God's covenant love for his children. David would know that God had come to Noah, Abraham and Moses and renewed his promise to them, a promise that he would be their God and would come to their aid whenever they needed help. If the rainbow had communicated to Noah that God remembered the promise that he had made (Gen. 9:16), everything that had happened since that time had confirmed it: God had not forsaken his children. In the midst of the most appalling difficulty I can say to myself, 'God remembers his covenant. His word will not fail. I have no need to worry.' No wonder David is full of praise!

Praise is about the last thing on our minds in difficult times, but praise is the key that unlocks the door that leads to a closer walk with God. David makes his vows of praise at the end of this psalm like this:

'Vows made to you are binding upon me, O God;
I will render praises to you,
For you have delivered my soul from death'

(vv. 12-13).

See if you cannot find something to praise God for in the time of your trouble!

Psalm 71

'In you, O Lord, I put my trust;
Let me never be put to shame.
Deliver me in your righteousness, and cause me to escape;
Incline your ear to me, and save me.
Be my strong habitation,
To which I may resort continually;
You have given the commandment to save me,
For you are my rock and my fortress.

Deliver me, O my God, out of the hand of the wicked,
Out of the hand of the unrighteous and cruel man.
For you are my hope, O Lord God;
You are my trust from my youth.
By you I have been upheld from my birth;
You are he who took me out of my mother's womb.
My praise shall be continually of you.

I have become as a wonder to many,
But you are my strong refuge.
Let my mouth be filled with your praise
And with your glory all the day.

Do not cast me off in the time of old age;
Do not forsake me when my strength fails.
For my enemies speak against me;
And those who lie in wait for my life take counsel together,
Saying, "God has forsaken him;
Pursue and take him, for there is none to deliver him."

O God, do not be far from me;
O my God, make haste to help me!
Let them be confounded and consumed
Who are adversaries of my life;
Let them be covered with reproach and dishonour
Who seek my hurt.

But I will hope continually,
And will praise you yet more and more.

My mouth shall tell of your righteousness
And your salvation all the day,
For I do not know their limits.
I will go in the strength of the Lord God;
I will make mention of your righteousness, of yours only.

O God, you have taught me from my youth;
And to this day I declare your wondrous works.
Now also when I am old and grey-headed,
O God, do not forsake me,
Until I declare your strength to this generation,
Your power to everyone who is to come.

Also your righteousness, O God, is very high,
You who have done great things;
O God, who is like you?
You, who have shown me great and severe troubles,
Shall revive me again,
And bring me up again from the depths of the earth.
You shall increase my greatness,
And comfort me on every side.

Also with the lute I will praise you;
And your faithfulness, O my God!
To you I will sing with the harp,
O Holy One of Israel.
My lips shall greatly rejoice when I sing to you,
And my soul, which you have redeemed.
My tongue also shall talk of your righteousness all the day long;
For they are confounded,
For they are brought to shame
Who seek my hurt.'

8.
A psalm for old age

Psalm 71

I once read of a sociologist who asked an eighteen-year-old, 'What do you think about old age?' and was given the answer: 'I hope to die before then.' Few want to think too deeply about old age and its problems.

Modern psychologists speak about 'the third age'. Our lives, so they say, can be divided into three 'ages': childhood, adulthood and retirement. Retirement, or 'the post-working life', as it is now sometimes called, is the 'third age'. Adjusting from one stage to another, passing through the two great turning-points in our life (childhood into adulthood, adulthood into retirement) sometimes gives rise to problems. The psalmist seems to know something of this when he cries out in this psalm: 'Do not cast me off in the time of old age' (v. 9), 'Now also when I am old and grey-headed, O God, do not forsake me...' (v. 18).

Feeling useless is something all of us fear who are anxious to give our lives to God's service. Here, in this psalm, the writer feels that there is so much more to do for God (vv. 16-17). What help is there for such a person? What does this psalm tell us about coping with the onset of old age? The answer lies in verse 14, when the psalmist says, 'But I will hope continually, and will praise you yet more and more.'

Perhaps you have noticed how the old can sometimes become difficult. Life has become a burden, and they feel themselves to be an even greater burden. This is where Psalm 71 is especially helpful.

Loss of joy

The thought emerges that, no matter what, we were made to praise God. Those who have come to know him as a Saviour (as the psalmist evidently had, v. 3) feel that now all they want to do, all they *can* do, is to praise him: 'Let my mouth be filled with your praise and with your glory all the day' (v. 8).

When the Reformers came to summarize Christianity in terms of 'glorifying God and enjoying him for ever' (the answer to the first question of the Shorter Catechism: 'What is man's chief end?') they were expressing an essentially biblical idea. 'Whoever offers praise glorifies me' (Ps. 50:23).

What Adam and Eve lost when they fell into sin was the joy of knowing God. Contrast their sense of shame and the evident burden of their existence after the Fall with their innocence and contentment before it (Gen.1:25; 3:8-10,17-19). When Paul summarizes all he knows of Christianity, he insists that joy is right there at the heart of it: 'The kingdom of God is ... righteousness and peace and joy in the Holy Spirit' (Rom. 14:17). Jesus too, giving his disciples final instructions before his departure, brings out joy as being of the essence of what the Christian life is all about. Praying to his Father, he says, 'But now I come to you, and these things I speak in the world, that they may have my joy fulfilled in themselves' (John 17:13).

Nehemiah too, seeing its value for practical purposes, insisted that strength springs from the felt joy in knowing God (Neh. 8:12). With work to be done in Jerusalem, this could hardly have been more relevant.

What the psalmist has come to realize in Psalm 71 is that we are at our best when adoring our Maker and Saviour. When there is no joy in our lives it usually means that we have taken our eyes off the Lord — something the psalmist felt tempted to do. Maybe it was the sharp pain of an arthritic hip, or the breathlessness he felt just trying to make his way about, or the grey hairs he saw in the reflection of his face from the bowl of water he used to wash.

His strength was failing him and he knew it (v. 9). With failing strength comes the feeling of uselessness; and with uselessness comes the loss of joy. That is why the psalmist insists on getting a hold on himself: self-pity is dangerously close at hand and he wants none of it. 'Fill me with praise,' he says, 'before I fall down this spiral of resentment and pity.'

Joy is what God wants us to experience.

Praise for what God has done

Another thought emerges: he has not praised God enough as yet. God's hand has been upon him since he was born (v. 6). Throughout his life God has been there: he has saved him (v. 3), defended him (being his 'rock', v. 3 and his 'refuge', v. 7). God is faithful (v. 22). There has not been a single moment when God has utterly forsaken him. Whenever there was trouble (and the psalmist confesses to times of severe trouble, v. 20) the Lord was always there to help and sustain him.

Think of it this way. Think of the time when you first caught a sight of your sins that separated you from God, and you were terrified that you should die in that hopeless condition, unfit to meet him who is holy and righteous and cannot clear those who are guilty (Exod. 34:7). Remember how you caught a further glimpse of God's Son dying in your place, suffering not on account of anything that he had done, but taking upon himself the punishment that your sins deserved. When you first placed your trust in Jesus as Lord and Saviour of your life and felt the burden of sins 'rolling away', was that not an experience full of joy? Did you not find that, at first, you were unable to keep this to yourself but felt constrained to tell others about it? How is it now? Is that joy still a part of your life?

What I am saying here is that the feeling of joy that springs from knowing God, and his love to those who have his Son as Saviour, must be expressed in praise. Thankfulness and joy are marriage partners. Over 140 references in the Bible underline the fact that thankfulness should be a priority in our lives. This thought emerges in one of Paul's exhortations: 'As you have therefore received Christ Jesus the Lord, so walk in him, rooted and built up in him and established in the faith, as you have been taught, abounding in it with thanksgiving' (Col. 2:6-7).

Then compare these verses from the psalms: 'Whoever offers praise glorifies me' (Ps. 50:23); 'It is good to give thanks to the Lord' (Ps.92:1); 'Enter into his gates with thanksgiving, and into his courts with praise' (Ps.100:4). 'Praise the Lord! Oh, give thanks to the Lord, for he is good! For his mercy endures for ever' (Ps.106:1-2).

Clearly, if the psalms tell us anything at all, they tell us that we haven't thanked God enough for what he has done for us. The thought that old age might rob him of the spirit of thankfulness terrifies the psalmist. His prayer ensures that it will not.

Counting our blessings

Another shade of colour emerges in this portrait of praise: we have
so much to thank God for:

'My mouth shall tell of your righteousness
And your salvation all the day,
For I do not know their limits'

(v.15).

It is almost as though the psalmist fears that old age may bring
a peculiar form of self-interest. Those who work with the elderly
confirm this. A spirit of thankfulness can often be in short supply,
and it is not hard to see why. The old have taken more knocks out
of life than anyone else; they have experienced most of what this
sinful world can hurl at them. Little wonder that they reach old age
bruised and battered. Only the Holy Spirit can keep God's children
from selfishness and self-pity, and the way he does that is by a
reminder of all that God has done — what Paul refers to as the 'width
and length and depth and height' of God's loving ways with his
children (Eph. 3:18).

Joy comes from knowing, as does the psalmist here, that God
loves him. Counting our blessings, naming them 'one by one', is the
advice of a well-known hymn, and good advice it is. What keeps us
sweet rather than sour is a reminder of just how much God has done
for us — and what he is yet going to do for us! As aspirin kills pain,
so a critical spirit kills joy. The antidote to a critical spirit, or to anger
at seeing younger folk taking on responsibility, or to the feeling of
being unwanted, forgotten, or lonely is to know that God has used
the old for some of his best works!

Moses had turned eighty when God showed himself to him in a
burning bush and called upon him to lead Israel out of Egypt (Exod.
3). Caleb was eighty-five when he entered into his inheritance (Josh.
14:6-15). Samuel was old when he established the 'school of the
prophets' (1 Sam. 8:5; 10:10; 12:2). Paul was an old man too when
he wrote 1 and 2 Timothy, without which we would be all the poorer
in our understanding of so many things. Keeping these things in
mind will keep our spirits sweet.

Sometimes we are not thankful, not because we are ungrateful,
but because we are far too conscious of the blessings we lack.

Problems cloud our vision and prevent praise. It is said that, on one occasion, the Cleveland Orchestra were playing the overture to *The Magic Flute* by Mozart when the house lights went out due to a power-failure. The orchestra kept playing and managed to reach the end — perfectly, or so the audience felt as they gave generous applause. Sometimes in our relationship with God it feels as though the lights have gone out (Isa. 50:10).We should know God so well that we are able to sing his praise in the dark!

Every time you are tempted to wonder as to the goodness of God, think of the cross. Where was the light when Jesus cried out, 'My God, my God, why have you forsaken me?' (Matt. 27:46). There was darkness all around, as the context makes clear, but far greater was the darkness within his own soul. You must admit, the idea that God's Son should be abandoned in this way is astonishing. Think of the nakedness, the terrible pain, the spit of soldiers in his face, the smell of sweat and blood and the mocking crowd. The storm grew and the crowds thinned, and Jesus was heard to cry to his Father. And heaven was silent!

Heaven accused Jesus of lust and lying ... covetousness and crime ... greed and godlessness! It is not that Jesus was guilty of any of these things — he was sinless (Matt. 27:4; 2 Cor. 5:21; 1 Peter 1:19). But heaven accused him in our place: 'For he made him who knew no sin to be sin for us, that we might become the righteousness of God in him' (2 Cor. 5:21).

Where was God's love in all this? It was there all along. God punished every one of our sins to the full that day so that he might never have to do so again. He punished his own Son, so that we might never have to suffer. That is how much he loved us. If that doesn't make you want to stand up and sing God's praise, nothing will!

How shall we praise God?

1. With effort

Self-exertion is essential: 'In you, O Lord, I put my trust' (v. 1); 'You are my hope...' (v. 5); 'I will hope continually, and will praise you yet more and more' (v. 14).You can almost see the psalmist shaking himself into a thankful response. Worship is hard work! So,

set to it and get started! The psalmist refuses to be drawn into the
attitude that we worship only when we feel like it. Nor is he waiting
for some extra experience to motivate him for worship. It is laziness,
and deep down it is sin, that keeps us from telling God how great he
is. Worship is hard work! Did you, I wonder, ever think of it that
way? One of my objections to modern worship is that it is too often
laid-back and informal. It takes no great energy to sing some of the
modern items of praise.

2. *With our whole hearts*

The psalmist is not content with anything less than wholehearted
worship (v. 8). This is the only way to tell God how much we love
him. One of my favourite Bible texts underlines the blessings of
wholehearted worship: 'And you will seek me and find me, when
you search for me with all your heart' (Jer. 29:13). There is nothing
at all mechanical about the way this man worships his God.

3. *With the best theology*

Rock-climbers secure their ropes to special pins called 'cleats'. By
means of these sophisticated pegs, they ascend higher and higher.
God's attributes are something like that.

We find, as we familiarize ourselves with God's hymn-book,
that the way to worship God is to remind ourselves, over and over
again, of who God is and what he is like. Just look at the list of
characteristics of God which this psalm underlines: he is righteous
(vv. 2, 16, 19, 24); he listens to prayer (v. 2), he is one in whom we
feel 'at home' (v.3), dependable and trustworthy (vv. 3, 7), the one
who looks after us every step of the journey to heaven (v. 6), glorious
(v. 8), a Saviour (v. 15), powerful (v. 18), a strengthener and
comforter (v. 21), faithful and holy (v. 22).

This is how theology is best learnt — in praise of God. This is
how we should worship God every time.

4. *With prayerfulness*

All the psalms are prayers. That is why believers down through the
ages have resorted to them again and again as models for their own
prayer lives and why many schemes for reading the Bible in a year

have the Bible divided in such a way that a psalm falls on every day. That is done for a purpose. God not only intends us to pray. He gives us models: the Lord's Prayer falls into this category; so do the prayers of godly men and women like Abraham, Moses, Hannah, Samuel, Daniel, Ezra and Paul, and so do the psalms of David.

Psalm 119, part 3

'Deal bountifully with your servant,
That I may live and keep your word.
Open my eyes, that I may see
Wondrous things from your law.
I am a stranger in the earth;
Do not hide your commandments from me.
My soul breaks with longing
For your judgements at all times.
You rebuke the proud; the cursed,
Who stray from your commandments.
Remove from me reproach and contempt,
For I have kept your testimonies.
Princes also sit and speak against me,
But your servant meditates on your statutes.
Your testimonies also are my delight
And my counsellors'

(vv. 17-24).

9.
How to get the best from your Bible

Psalm 119, part 3

We have already seen how 'God's alphabet psalm' is designed to promote holiness. The way it does this is to focus our attention upon God's Word, the Bible. Turning the spotlight on section 3 of the psalm (vv. 17-24) highlights three things we need to do in order to get the best from our Bibles.

1. We must pray for light

I must confess that I'm not very good at those 'do-it-yourself' projects that need doing around the house. I can turn my hand to some things, but others I have to leave for the experts.

Electricity frightens me. I'm not sure why, but I think it is because you cannot see it. Don't misunderstand me! I can change a plug and even attempt something a little more complicated. But when it comes to wiring, I'm baffled. 'Light' is something I had not had in my garage for over a year! The strip-lighting was broken one day by an over-ambitious attempt at an overhand yorker with my son. I always meant to fix it, but never got around to it. Part of the problem lay in the fact that it needed more than just a new bulb. It needed completely rewiring! That was something I was reluctant to do.

As I said, it was over a year before I attempted to fix it. It was after tripping over various objects and one bruised leg in particular that I summoned up the resolve to attempt to fix the light. It didn't work! No matter how carefully I put the wires together, no light came. It was then I called one of the deacons (a former electrician!) and in less than a minute he was able to show me that my wiring was incorrect! Since then, I have been able to see my way into the garage, and the study that lies at the back of it.

Clearly, light is important. The very first thing God created after he made the earth was light (Gen.1:3). We were never meant to be creatures of the dark.

Light, of a different kind, is what we need, to know and worship God. Chrysostom, writing in the fourth century, once wrote, 'Like men with sore eyes: they find the light painful, while the darkness, which permits them to see nothing, is restful and agreeable.'[1] Fallen man is at home in the dark. He prefers darkness to light. Christians are different; they have been brought out of darkness and into light: 'For you were once darkness, but now you are light in the Lord' (Eph. 5:8); 'You are all sons of light and sons of the day. We are not of the night nor of darkness' (1 Thess. 5:5).

Walking in the light is *living by the Bible.* Psalm 119 is anxious to elicit from us a love for the Bible and what it has to say to us: 'Open my eyes, that I may see wondrous things from your law' (v.18). Even the apostles needed light to understand what they themselves were writing! The apostle Peter makes the most startling admission in the last few written words we have from his pen: there are some things in Paul's letters that are difficult to understand! (2 Peter 3:15-16). Not all the Bible is equally clear. God has given us a map to show us the way from the gates of hell to the gates of heaven, but in order to read it, we need light. This is what theologians refer to as the illumination of the Holy Spirit. But before we take a look at the word 'illumination' we need to glance at another: 'perspicuity'.

First, let me quote from the *Westminster Confession of Faith:* 'All things in Scripture are not alike plain in themselves, nor alike clear unto all: yet those things which are necessary to be known, believed, and observed for salvation, are so clearly propounded, and opened in some place of Scripture or other, that not only the learned, but the unlearned, in a due use of the ordinary means, may attain unto a sufficient understanding of them.'[2]

That is the classic statement on the perspicuity of Scripture. But what is 'perspicuity'? What does the word mean? Perhaps if we used instead the word 'clarity' we might have a better appreciation of its significance. God's Word is a light to all who read it. Everyone who reads the Bible can appreciate some light emerging from it.

Traditionally, three verses from Psalm 119 have been used to justify this statement of doctrine:

'I will praise you with uprightness of heart,
When I learn your righteous judgements'

(v.7).

'Your word is a lamp to my feet
And a light to my path'

(v.105).

'The entrance of your words gives light;
It gives understanding to the simple'

(v.130).

When men wrote the Bible they wrote for fellow believers, and what they wrote was intended to be understood by them. It is true that Jesus did say something about speaking in parables so that those who heard them might *not* understand (Mark 4:11-12). And we have already alluded to Peter's comment about some of Paul's writings (2 Peter 3:15-16). And we have all, at some time or another, found that a study of the Bible has left us more confused than ever!

The Reformers were anxious to underline the statement of the perspicuity of Scripture because of another equally important doctrine related to it: the priesthood of all believers. The Bible is a book for the people. Tyndale's vision that the common ploughman should be able to read it, and understand its central message, was governed by this very truth. Though there may be *parts* of the Bible which are difficult, taken as a whole it is not.

Eight times Psalm 119 refers to understanding the Word of God (vv. 34, 73, 99, 104, 125, 130, 144, 169). Two things are needed to make Scripture clear: a saving relationship with Jesus Christ and the illuminating work of the Holy Spirit.

When Philip sat up in the chariot of the Chancellor of Queen Candace, he was speaking to a man who was absorbed by the Bible, but knew nothing of its perspicuity. 'Do you understand what you are reading?' Philip asked (Acts 8:30). Clearly, the man did not. It was by expounding Isaiah 53, with its references to Jesus Christ and his atoning work (what Luke refers to as 'preaching Jesus to him', Acts 8:35) that the man began to understand the Scriptures.

Knowing Christ in his capacity as Lord and Saviour is essential in order to understand the Bible. Christ is the hub in which all the spokes of biblical teaching meet. Without knowing him we shall make few advances in our understanding of Scripture.

In addition to a saving relationship with Jesus Christ, we shall also need the illuminating work of the Holy Spirit if we are to understand our Bibles. The Holy Spirit is, after all, Christ's representative in our hearts. He was sent 'in Jesus' name' (John 14:6), as the Father's agent (15:26; 16:7), to be with Jesus' disciples for ever (14:16), thereby bringing Jesus' ministry 'back' to them again (14:18-23). The disciples on the Emmaus road saw Christ in the Scriptures, but it was Christ himself who showed himself to have been there in the Bible all along. It is precisely this ministry which is promised to all Christians. The Holy Spirit shines a light on the Scriptures, an essential requirement if we are ever to make 'sense' of the Bible.

2. We need a good appetite

Another requirement in order to get the best from our Bibles is a good appetite for it.

> 'My soul breaks with longing
> For your judgements at all times'
>
> (v.20).
>
> 'Behold, I long for your precepts;
> Revive me in your righteousness'
>
> (v.40).
>
> 'I long for your salvation, O Lord,
> And your law is my delight'
>
> (v.174).

Loss of appetite is a classic symptom that all is not well. In the spiritual realm it is the same. There is a sticker which sometimes appears on the back-windscreens of cars, which reads, 'Have you read your Bible today?' Neglecting Bible reading is a sign that something is wrong.

This was the problem with the Hebrew Christians of the New Testament: 'For though by this time you ought to be teachers, you need someone to teach you again the first principles of the oracles of God; and you have come to need milk and not solid food. For everyone who partakes only of milk is unskilled in the word of righteousness, for he is a babe. But solid food belongs to those who are of full age, that is, those who by reason of use have their senses exercised to discern both good and evil' (Heb. 5:12-14).

Later on, the writer points out the reason for their lack of growth. Using the figure of a race, he suggests that some were trying to run with excessive weight (12:1). It is as though he were urging the need for a diet! The things in question may well be perfectly legitimate, but they are not helpful in a long-distance race. It is a bit like trying to run a marathon in a pair of Wellington boots! Then again, he goes on to suggest that some were breaking the rules of the race. They were not only to 'lay aside every weight', but they were also to lay aside the 'sin which so easily ensnares'.

3. We must let the Bible read us!

In an interesting reference, the psalmist likens the Bible to a counsellor: 'Your testimonies also are my delight and my counsellors' (v. 24). Whether we are willing to admit it or not, we all need help from time to time. Christian counsellors can be a source of great help to Christians in difficulty. The Bible encourages us to use the Scriptures as a source of help.

The psalm gives us at least five pictures to describe what the Bible is like.

1. A basin of clean water

'How can a young man cleanse his way?
By taking heed according to your word'

(v.9).

In the Old Testament tabernacle, there was a bronze laver filled with clean water, resting on a pedestal (Exod. 38:8). Here, the priests would stop and wash as ceremony demanded. Washing became a symbol of how sins are removed, telling us in effect that the Bible's four-letter word for sin is d-i-r-t! David cried,

'Wash me thoroughly from my iniquity,
And cleanse me from my sin...
Purge me with hyssop, and I shall be clean;
Wash me, and I shall be whiter than snow'

(Ps. 51:2,7).

This is, in part, what baptism pictures, and what spiritual rebirth confirms in the New Testament (John 3:5).

2. A tonic

'My soul clings to the dust;
Revive me according to your word'

(v.25).

'My soul melts from heaviness;
Strengthen me according to your word'

(v.28).

'This is my comfort in my affliction,
For your word has given me life'

(v.50).

'I will never forget your precepts,
For by them you have given me life'

(v.93).

'I am afflicted very much;
Revive me, O Lord, according to your word'

(v.107).

'Uphold me according to your word, that I may live;
And do not let me be ashamed of my hope'

(v.116).

When I was young I remember being given cod-liver oil as a tonic. I can taste the foul smell yet, and hear my mother assuring me that it was 'good for me'! God's Word is designed to make us better: healthy, strong and fit for any task.

3. A sweetener

'How sweet are your words to my taste,
Sweeter than honey to my mouth!'

(v.103).

Today, we are told that sugar is bad for us. Even the lowly can of baked beans now comes labelled: 'No added sugar'! According to Mary Poppins, 'A spoonful of sugar helps the medicine go down.' In life's trials there are many bitter pills to swallow. A spoonful of the Bible's rich promises will be a wonderful source of help.

4. A lamp

'Your word is a lamp to my feet
And a light to my path...
The entrance of your words gives light;
It gives understanding to the simple'

(vv.105, 130).

We have already seen how the Bible is like a torch to show us the way. My in-laws live just a stone's throw from Donaghadee lighthouse. On a foggy night its searching light pierces the darkest gloom. In the same way, the Bible penetrates into the thick darkness of our trials.

5. A very great treasure

'I rejoice at your word
As one who finds great treasure'

(v.162).

C. S. Lewis, in his book *The Voyage of the Dawn Treader* (one of the *Chronicles of Narnia*), tells how Lucy, Edmund and some others join Prince Caspian on a dangerous sea voyage in search of Prince Caspian's father's seven lost friends. On a certain island, they come to a place where a secret underground pool turns everything to gold. As soon as the secret is discovered, the friends begin to quarrel. It is a wonderful insight into the danger of riches. Instead of calling the island Goldwater Island, they call it Deathwater.[3]

Treasure can be ruinous; but not the treasure which the Bible gives. Getting the best from our Bibles means reading it, eagerly, with the help of the Holy Spirit, letting it analyse our hearts and motivate us to a closer walk with God.

Have you read your Bible this way today?

Psalm 92

'It is good to give thanks to the Lord,
And to sing praises to your name, O Most High;
To declare your loving-kindness in the morning,
And your faithfulness every night,
On an instrument of ten strings,
On the lute,
And on the harp,
With harmonious sound.
For you, Lord, have made me glad through your work;
I will triumph in the works of your hands.

O Lord, how great are your works!
Your thoughts are very deep.
A senseless man does not know,
Nor does a fool understand this.
When the wicked spring up like grass,
And when all the workers of iniquity flourish,
It is that they may be destroyed for ever.

But you, Lord, are on high for evermore.
For behold, your enemies, O Lord,
For behold, your enemies shall perish;
All the workers of iniquity shall be scattered.

But my horn you have exalted like a wild ox;
I have been anointed with fresh oil.
My eye also has seen my desire on my enemies;
My ears hear my desire on the wicked
Who rise up against me.

The righteous shall flourish like a palm tree,
He shall grow like a cedar in Lebanon.
Those who are planted in the house of the Lord
Shall flourish in the courts of our God.
They shall still bear fruit in old age;
They shall be fresh and flourishing,
To declare that the Lord is upright;
He is my rock, and there is no unrighteousness in him.'

10.
A song for the sabbath day

Psalm 92

The psalms are meant to help us. In this book we have seen how Psalm 5 encourages us to pray, Psalm 25 teaches us the value of spiritual meditation, Psalm 54 helps us to recover after a fall and Psalm 71 provides us with advice about getting old and staying joyful.

Psalm 92 gives us encouragement to *worship*. Part of our problem lies in the fact that we are too prone to look at ourselves rather than God. Worship is what we were made for, and our lives become unhinged when true worship is neglected.

Reading the small print

Psalm 92 is one of those psalms with a title. Publishers are very careful about titles! They need to convey what the book is about, but they also need to be eye-catching. Whether or not the title to Psalm 92 is 'eye-catching' is debatable, but it does set the picture of what the psalm is all about. Reading the 'small print' is always advisable. The title is found in the small print at the head of the psalm, and reads: 'A psalm: a song, for the sabbath day'. Every Lord's Day is a day of worship. It is a provision of God that every seventh day we take stock of our lives and gather collectively for worship. And worship is designed to help us get things into proper perspective. How many times, for example, have problems diminished as we focused our attention on the character of God?

'It is good to give thanks to the Lord,
And to sing praises to your name, O Most High;

To declare your lovingkindness in the morning,
And your faithfulness every night'

(Ps. 92:1-2).

This is how the psalm begins, setting the tone immediately as one of joy and gladness at the very thought of another sabbath.

What is so wonderful about this psalm in the sense of joy it conveys in the Lord's Day. The argument runs something like this: the Lord's Day is when we gather for worship. Worship involves coming into God's presence and appreciating just how wonderful he is. In fact, worship is doing what we were made to do. And there is no joy to be found anywhere to compare with the sense of real satisfaction gained by doing what we were meant to do. That's why real worship is an occasion of real joy. This is what the psalmist is trying to convey here.

Isaac Watts paraphrased these sentiments this way:

Sweet is the work, my God and King
To praise thy name, give thanks and sing
To show thy love by morning light
And talk of all thy truth at night

Sweet is the day of sacred rest
No mortal cares shall seize my breast
Oh, may my heart in tune be found
Like David's harp of solemn sound!

What worship involves

One of the things this psalm helps us to understand is how to worship God. Six key words come into focus.

1. Reverence

'But you, Lord, are on high for evermore' (v. 8). The psalm is full of praise, but it is reverent praise. It is concerned with God — his attributes and his works.

Worship must always be reverential: 'Oh come, let us worship and bow down, let us kneel before the Lord our Maker' (Ps. 95:6).

It is the response of a redeemed sinner to the holiness of God. 'Give unto the Lord the glory due to his name; worship the Lord in the beauty of holiness' (Ps. 29:2).

The seraphim worship this way, too, continually crying, 'And one cried to another and said: "Holy, holy, holy is the Lord of hosts; the whole earth is full of his glory!"' (Isa. 6:3). So overwhelmed are they at the sight of God's holiness that they cover their eyes with their wings.

Holiness conveys the idea of just how different God is from the rest of creation. Think of his greatness and power in contrast with man's smallness and weakness; think, too, of his purity and uprightness in contrast to man's unrighteousness and sinfulness. It is because of God's purity that evil-doers will be destroyed (v. 7). It is because of God's purity that Jesus whipped tradesmen out of the temple (Mark 11:15-17; John 2:14-16) and hurled verbal vitriol at the arrogant, but hypocritical, church leaders of his day (Matt. 23); and cursed the fig tree as a sign of his displeasure at unfaithful Israel (Mark 11:12-14, 20-24).

2. Seriousness

The psalmist considers the fate of the wicked and reminds us of their eventual destruction:

'When the wicked spring up like grass,
And when all the workers of iniquity flourish,
It is that they may be destroyed for ever'

(v. 7).

Thoughts like these are accompanied by great solemnity. You cannot be flippant and speak of hell at the same time!

Nowhere in Scripture is true worship ever portrayed in other than serious terms. Thus A. W. Pink could say that worship is 'the adoration of a redeemed people, occupied with God himself'. It is serious because it is unlike anything else that we do. Worship is for God alone.

Today we are constantly being told that worship should be 'informal'. Evangelistic meetings encourage informality instead of confronting sinners with the seriousness of sin and the seriousness of worship. People are not encouraged to sing David's psalms, or even the great serious hymns composed in days of revival. Little wonder that sinners leave meetings thinking that God can be trifled with.

God complained in the Old Testament that the false prophets were causing his people 'to err by their lies, and by their lightness' (Jer. 23:32, AV). The Puritan David Clarkson, in a sermon entitled 'Public worship to be preferred before private', speaks of the sense of God's presence in worship: 'The most wonderful things that are now done on earth are wrought in the public ordinances. Here the dead hear the voice of the Son of God, and those that hear do live ... Here he cures diseased souls with a word ... Here he disposes Satan ... Wonders they are, and would be so accounted, were they not the common work of the public ministry.'[1] This is what our worship should be like: full of God's felt presence.

3. Adoration

'It is good to give thanks to the Lord...' (v.1). The English word 'worship' is derived from the Elizabethan word 'worthwhile'. To worship is to say with the psalmist, 'Great is the Lord, and greatly to be praised; and his greatness is unsearchable' (Ps. 145:3). 'For I proclaim the name of the Lord: ascribe greatness to our God' (Deut. 32:3).

Worship is in essence giving glory to God:

'Give unto the Lord, O you mighty ones,
Give unto the Lord glory and strength.
Give unto the Lord the glory due to his name;
Worship the Lord in the beauty of holiness'

(Ps. 29:1,2).

The book of Revelation continually ascribes glory to God: 'To him be glory and dominion for ever and ever. Amen' (Rev. 1:6; cf.4:9,11; 5:12-13; 7:12; 11:13; 14:7; 15:4,8; 19:1,7; 21:11,23).

Worship is, according to the second verse, showing forth the lovingkindness of God in the morning and his faithfulness at night. The New International Version uses the verb 'to proclaim' instead of 'showing forth' here, as it does again in verse 15 — this time speaking of the elderly, too frail to gather with the rest, yet still 'proclaiming, "The Lord is upright; he is my rock, and there is no wickedness in him."'

Worship is, essentially, the reverse of sin. Sin makes ourselves the centre of all things, whereas worship makes God all-important. True worship is a celebration of God in praise, prayer and proclamation. Wesley, in his 'Rules for Methodist singers', had this to say about singing in public worship: 'Above all, sing spiritually. Have an eye to God in every word you sing. Aim at pleasing him more than yourself or any other creature. In order to do this, attend strictly to the sense of what you sing, and see that your heart is not carried away with the sound, but offered to God continually.'[2]

4. Truthfulness

When the psalmist says in the closing verse, 'There is no unrighteousness in him' (v. 15), he is stating the fact that God is always true to himself. He never deviates from the given standard — which is himself! That means that worship must be righteous. It must be 'according to rule'. It must be true worship!

Jesus told the woman of Samaria that true worship is from the heart, through the Holy Spirit and in accordance with the truth of the gospel (John 4:19-21,24). True worship is offered only by those whose hearts have been renewed, justified by faith alone in Christ alone, and who now live in meek submission to his Word. 'For we are the circumcision, who worship God in the Spirit, rejoice in Christ Jesus, and have no confidence in the flesh' (Phil. 3:3). True worship is always according to truth.

Christians never honour God more than when they listen reverently to his Word being proclaimed, intending not just to hear but to obey. Current expectations about preaching are low. That is a reflection on both modern preaching and modern listening! Far too often Christians rebel at having to think. Mindless worship is the cult of the day and we yield to it at our great peril! 'Don't be like a beast, but use your minds' is God's plea in Psalm 32. He still pleads thus today.

5. Joyfulness

'It is good to praise the Lord and make music to your name, O Most High' (Ps. 92:1, NIV). Man's chief end is to glorify God and to enjoy him for ever. Sinners who are restored to fellowship with God are conscious of a sense of satisfaction unequalled by anything this world affords:

'Thus I will bless you while I live;
I will lift up my hands in your name.
My soul shall be satisfied as with marrow and fatness,
And my mouth shall praise you with joyful lips'

(Ps. 63:4-5).

Partly, this joy is due to what we know to be true in ourselves: we are no longer what we were — we are a new creation (2 Cor. 5:17). Sin has been forgiven, justification acquired and adoption bestowed. Partly, too, it is because every Christian feels whenever he worships God that somehow he is sharing in the powers of the world to come (Heb. 6:5). Sometimes, we are conscious of being in another world — of being in the very presence of God.

In a staggeringly off-hand remark about prophecy, Paul states that unbelievers on hearing it will 'worship God and report that God is truly among you' (1 Cor. 14:25). Knowing God's presence in this way is a joyful, if humbling experience.

Discovering ourselves, finding out exactly what it is the Lord made us for, is a joyful experience: 'I sing for joy at the work of your hands' (v. 4, NIV).

Joy was something for which our Lord prayed in the high priestly prayer: 'But now I come to you, and these things I speak in the world, that they may have my joy fulfilled in themselves' (John 17:13). In the Old Testament the word 'joy' occurs several hundred times. In the New Testament the verb occurs seventy-two times and the noun over sixty! The Bible is all about finding 'solid joys and lasting treasures'! Joy is one of the blessings of true Christian worship.

David was not a man who simply wrote poetry to pass the time of day. He is telling us just how much worship can affect our lives. He was, after all, a king with all the pressures and burdens of state, who had fought lions and bears, faced Goliath and withstood the megalomaniac Saul. David had had his share of problems.

Yet David had also grown in grace. Every day that went by, he knew something more about God. Listen to him shout in the eighth verse: 'But you, O Lord, are exalted for ever' (NIV). God was greater than any of David's problems. He refused to sit in the corner and feel sorry for himself. No matter what, God is worthy to be praised.

One of the wonderful things about this psalm is the way it speaks quite frankly about our secret fears. Who of us hasn't thought about our future? If we are spared to old age will it mean senility? Will we deny the Lord?

'The righteous shall flourish like a palm tree,
He shall grow like a cedar in Lebanon.
Those who are planted in the house of the Lord
Shall flourish in the courts of our God.
They shall still bear fruit in old age;
They shall be fresh and flourishing'

(vv.12-14).

As we have seen, this is not the first time we come across David contemplating old age in the psalms. In Psalm 71 (which could well be called 'A psalm for old age') he cries, 'Do not cast me off in the time of old age; do not forsake me when my strength fails' (v. 9). Old age brings many problems, but it also brings many opportunities. It is a time when the realization of the promises of God is that much nearer. Even when the outward man decays (and none of us is promised freedom from that) the inward man goes on being renewed day by day.

6. Service

'They shall still bear fruit in old age,' the psalmist confidently assures us. Bearing fruit is the result of true worship.

Two of the most important Greek words for worship are words which basically mean 'service'. One (*leitourgia*) was taken from secular life where it denoted service rendered 'free of charge' to the community. Worship is a life freely offered to God: 'I beseech you therefore, brethren, by the mercies of God, that you present your bodies a living sacrifice, holy, acceptable to God, which is your reasonable service' (Rom. 12:1). This is the only way really to worship God — giving ourselves utterly to him, wholeheartedly, as did Caleb (Num. 14:24; Deut. 1:36), Joshua the son of Nun (Num. 32:12; Josh. 14:8), Hezekiah (2 Chr. 31:21), and the Christians in the church at Rome (Rom. 6:17).

Worship is well summed up in the words of the sweet and godly Miss Havergal: 'Take my life, and let it be consecrated, Lord, to thee.'

Awe, wonder, profound joy, a sense of privilege — these are the emotions the psalmist felt every time he gathered for worship on the sabbath day. Do you ever feel as overcome as this? What was it that caused Isaiah or John to fall down in astonishment in the presence of God? (Isa. 6; Rev. 1). Why do we feel today the need to introduce items of entertainment into worship in order to 'liven it up'? Young people need 'Christian' rock bands, we are told. An older generation seems to need the same kind of thing, perhaps with country-and-western style singers replacing the heavy metal. Are we not able, any more, to reflect upon the Lord and be moved to worship?

True, the psalmist used a 'ten-stringed instrument'. But read the psalm again and see if you do not agree with me that the entire emphasis falls upon God. It is the Lord who is central. He dominates everything. The psalmist is taken up entirely with telling God how great he is!

Have you ever got up in the morning and before doing anything else thought about God's love? Evidently the psalmist had (v. 2).

Love and faithfulness: a summary of God's character

The word used here for 'love' *(hesed)* occurs frequently in the psalms and more or less summarizes the entire message of the Bible. It is God's covenant love. It is often translated 'loving-kindness' in the Authorized Version.

This love is beautifully captured in the words of Jonathan to David: 'And you shall not only show me the kindness of the Lord while I still live, that I may not die' (1 Sam. 20:14). When Abraham's servant was sent to find a wife for Isaac we can imagine how perplexed he must have felt when he stopped at the well in Nahor for a drink of water! In times of difficulty, God's people have always found comfort in recalling God's unceasing kindness in helping his children. Thus the servant prayed that day, 'Then he said, "O Lord God of my master Abraham, please give me success this day, and show kindness to my master Abraham"' (Gen. 24:12). Thus it was, too, that Solomon, overcome by his responsibilities as head of state and conscious of his own inadequacies, prayed, 'And Solomon said: "You have shown great mercy to your servant David my father ... Therefore give to your servant an understanding heart to judge your people..."' (1 Kings 3:6,9).

Early in the morning we are to think of how God has established
a relationship of love with us, restoring us into fellowship with him
through his own Son's sacrificial, substitutionary atoning death. It
is a relationship sovereignly established which cannot be broken.

If you are a Christian, God loves you with unfailing love! Did
you, this morning, tell him how much you loved him in return?

We can depend upon God's love. Having saved us, he is
determined to stay with us (even if that means a rebuke every now
and then). If in the morning we can depend upon his love to help us
face the day, then in the evening we can turn to him again and thank
him for his faithfulness in keeping his word.

What better time is there to think about God's faithfulness than
in the evening? Another day has passed in which God has kept his
word, provided for us and helped us. Love and faithfulness are
marriage partners. The one explains the other. They occur together
in many of the psalms (36:5; 57:3; 61:7; 85:10; 86:15; 89:14; 115:1;
138:2).

The heart of consecrated living is spending the entire day in the
conscious presence of God: 'in the morning ... in the evening...' Is
this how you spend each day?

Tell God how much he means to you, how great he is and how
meaningless life would be without him. Tell him how encouraging
it is to know his arms wrapped around you. Tell him!

I hate getting into a bed that hasn't been made! Obviously the
Puritan William Gurnall, author of *The Christian in Complete Ar-
mour*, did too, for he once wrote, 'He that takes no care to set forth
God's portion of time in the morning, doth not only rob God of his
due, but is a thief to himself all the day after, by losing the blessing
which a faithful prayer might bring from heaven on his undertak-
ings. And he that closeth his eyes at night without prayer, lies down
before his bed is made.'

Laudate et superexaltate eum in saeculo! — Praise him and
magnify him for ever!

It is good to praise the Lord (v. 1). Discovering just how
delightful worship can be is one of the best things we can ever do.
Take a note of just how radiant the psalmist is: he sings (v. 1); he
makes melody (v. 3); he is glad (v. 4).

It is not too far-fetched to say that the psalmist has found himself.
He has discovered the reason for his existence: to worship God! The
world is full of people whose sadness is self-evident. They are lost.

They do not know why they are here. It is only when we worship the Lord that we are truly human. In a world that is crying out for that ultimate experience, the psalmist quietly and confidently tells us that it is to be found on our knees, worshipping the Lord!

Psalm 119, part 4

'This is my comfort in my affliction,
For your word has given me life'

(v. 50).

'Before I was afflicted I went astray,
But now I keep your word'

(v. 67).

'It is good for me that I have been afflicted,
That I may learn your statutes'

(v. 71).

'I know, O Lord, that your judgements are right,
And that in faithfulness you have afflicted me'

(v. 75).

'Unless your law had been my delight,
I would then have perished in my affliction'

(v. 92).

'I am afflicted very much;
Revive me, O Lord, according to your word'

(v. 107).

'Consider my affliction and deliver me,
For I do not forget your law'

(v. 153).

11.
When the Lord strikes

Psalm 119, part 4

'I believe faith will teach you to kiss a striking Lord ... If our dear Lord pluck up one of his roses, and pull down sour and green fruit before harvest, who can challenge him? ... Your Husbandman and Lord hath lopped off some branches already ... All these crosses ... are to make you white and ripe for the Lord's harvest-hook.'[1] These words were written in 1634 by Samuel Rutherford to Lady Kenmure on the death of her daughter. Having known much suffering himself, he was able to help others in their sorrow.

Seven times in Psalm 119 we are told that here is a man who knows about suffering (vv. 50, 67, 71, 75, 92, 107, 153). 'I am afflicted very much,' he cries (v. 107).

Several things account for it, including the general godlessness of his age and the mocking he receives for his faith (vv. 51, 53). What is of interest to us here, however, is his overall assessment of the benefit suffering has brought into his life: 'It is good for me,' he testifies, 'that I have been afflicted' (v. 71). Only those who have walked closely with God have learnt to see suffering this way. What can this possibly mean?

Anyone who has been brought up short only to find out that their fellowship with God has been out of sorts will come to see that, in the long run, it is a good thing. Whatever the difficulty may be, we may be sure that a loving purpose lies behind it. As King Hezekiah said, 'Surely it was for my benefit that I suffered such anguish' (Isa. 38:17, NIV). The Lord never acts capriciously. Jeremiah wrote,

'Though he causes grief,
Yet he will show compassion
According to the multitude of his mercies.

For he does not afflict willingly,
Nor grieve the children of men'

(Lam. 3:32-33).

The psalmist gives his own testimony: he has tasted 'the good life', only to find that it led him astray (v. 67). Having felt the rod of correction, he is grateful, for it has brought him closer to God.

Sometimes we are so slow to learn God's lessons. Patient appeals seem on occasion to be inadequate. Only the sting of a sharp blow wakes us up to the urgency of our need. The sting of affliction, when responded to in a mature way, aids the process of renewing fellowship with God. It is not always so, of course. Correction can make people bitter and resentful. The book of Hebrews suggests that 'many' are 'defiled' by the presence of problems in their lives (Heb. 12:15). Clearly, we need instruction as to how we are to cope with difficulties.

Correction

'Correction!' The word has such a negative ring to it. Yet how important it is! Solomon gave it a place of great prominence:

'My son, do not despise the chastening of the Lord,
Nor detest his correction'

(Prov. 3:11).

'Poverty and shame will come to him who disdains correction,
But he who regards reproof will be honoured'

(Prov. 13:18).

'Harsh correction is for him who forsakes the way,
And he who hates reproof will die'

(Prov. 15:10).

'Understanding is a wellspring of life to him who has it.
But the correction of fools is folly'

(Prov. 16:22).

'Foolishness is bound up in the heart of a child,
But the rod of correction will drive it far from him'

(Prov. 22:15).

'Do not withhold correction from a child,
For if you beat him with a rod, he will not die'

(Prov. 23:13).

Clearly, correction is something we all need 'from the cradle to the grave'.

David discovered this truth about himself and it was an alarming truth! It is something which, as Christians, we become aware of at an early stage in our spiritual life: despite having received the greatest of spiritual blessings, we can sometimes live for a period as though we had not! Discovering this truth is a most humbling and shameful experience.

As we saw earlier, there seems to have been a time when David lived apart from God. We find him lying to King Saul and the priests at Nob and playing the fool in Gath (1 Sam. 20; 21). During this period there is a curious omission in the account of his life with God. There is no mention of him praying. David was a fugitive, both from Saul and God. Running away from Saul led him to run away from God too. As A. W. Pink observes, 'When communion is broken, when the soul is out of touch with God, temptation is yielded unto and grievous sin is committed. It was so here.'[2] Then, suddenly, as though David has said to himself, 'What a fool I've been to live this way!' he seems to begin an exhilarating life of prayer: 'Therefore David enquired of the Lord, saying...' (1 Sam. 23:2; cf. 23:4; 28:6; 30:8; 2 Sam. 2:1; 5:19; 5:23).

Affliction taught David the value of prayer. 'Before I was afflicted I went astray, but now I keep your word' (v. 67). Others, too, have found this to be true. God uses affliction to loosen our hold on things that ultimately are of no value. Jim Elliot, shortly before he was murdered, wrote, 'I am willing that my house on earth be emptier [if only] his house be fuller.'

Learning that without God we 'can do nothing' (John 15:5) is often a painful process. We are apt to rely upon our own powers and abilities. We often deceive ourselves that we can get out of every tight corner. If, as Charles Colson suggests, the American national anthem is Frank Sinatra's 'I did it my way',[3] this is also the theme-song of those who stray from God.

Paul found this to be true. His afflictions were 'far beyond our ability to endure' (2 Cor. 1:8, NIV). Yet, he learnt that God has a purpose to fulfil in our lives — in the apostle's case this was 'that we should not trust in ourselves but in God who raises the dead' (v. 9).

God uses affliction to mould his children into a shape that is most useful for him. Learning to be pliable in the hands of God is what 'growing in grace' means. And grace, so Samuel Rutherford once remarked from a prison cell, 'grows best in winter'.[4]

The pruning knife

The Bible's word for this process is 'pruning': 'Every branch in me that does not bear fruit he takes away; and every branch that bears fruit he prunes, that it may bear more fruit' (John 15:2).

This is what reassures Job: he has felt the pain of pruning; now he longs for the new growth to appear:

'For there is hope for a tree,
If it is cut down, that it will sprout again,
And that its tender shoots will not cease.
Though its root may grow old in the earth,
And its stump may die in the ground,
Yet at the scent of water it will bud
And bring forth branches like a plant'

(Job 14:7-9).

This realization only came to Job after a hard struggle with God's providence. God is under no obligation to explain what he is doing in our lives. In the introduction to the book of Job we find ourselves overhearing a conversation between God and Satan. Clearly, there are immense theological problems in this scene. Although we are informed that God 'allows' his children to be tested by the devil, he never once satisfies our curiosity as to *why* he does so.

In fact, Job asks the question 'why?' sixteen times (Job 3:11,12,16,20,23; 7:20,21; 9:29; 10:2,18; 13:14,24; 24:1). Job is persistent in his desire to know why God is treating him in this way. But God does not answer him directly. There is a hint at the very end of the book that Job has come into a deeper relationship with God through his difficulties: 'I have heard of you by the hearing of the ear, but now my eye sees you,' he says (Job 42:5). The psalmist, too, seems to hint that he found the trial a questioning time, and had it not been for God's promises he would have sunk beneath the waves of his affliction (v. 92).

Affliction can deepen our relationship with God. Those who are suffering cry out more, plead more, pray more. As in the case of Jacob, an arthritic hip can be a constant reminder of our dependence upon God and a reminder, too, of former dealings with him (Gen. 32:22-32).

Sick patients in hospital often develop a bond with caring and devoted nurses, and are often able to confide with them more intimately than with their husbands or wives. The same God whose providence brings pain also heartens, helps and heals. Thus here, too, the psalmist confesses that in the midst of his troubles, God's Word has given him 'life' (v. 50), that everything God does is 'right' (v. 75) and that he will show his 'merciful kindness' (v. 76) and 'tender mercies' (v. 77).

Jerry Bridges tells the tale of the Crecopia moth, which in the process of emerging from its cocoon, undergoes an enormous struggle. A scientist, wanting to relieve the poor creature of the painful struggle, tried to help by gently cutting away part of the lining of the cocoon with a pair of scissors. The moth emerged crippled and useless. In the struggle to free itself, vital fluids are pumped into the outer reaches of the moth's wings. In trying to help, the scientist had in fact prevented this vital process.[5] God sometimes sends affliction to make us grow strong. Without it, we too can become weak and useless.

Learning to see things differently

Affliction sometimes teaches us to appreciate the truth that God does not always work in the way we expect him to. We may anticipate one way and God may act in another (Isa. 55:8). That seems to be what the psalmist is saying here when he says in verse 71, 'It is good for me that I have been afflicted, that I may learn your statutes.' It is almost as though he had become aware that God works in the most unexpected of ways. He can often surprise us that way.

Take the case of the blind man in Mark 8. He came to Jesus for healing. His case was genuine. But it is what Jesus did with him that is of interest. He took him by the hand to the edge of the village and then did a very strange thing. He spat in the man's eye! Whichever way you look at it, that is a very strange thing. I doubt if many of us would take that from anyone. Apart from anything else, Jesus was surely teaching this man a profound lesson: that blessing sometimes comes in the way we least expect it.

Maybe as you read these pages you too are feeling badly hurt. Maybe you feel a little angry with the way God has dealt with you. 'I deserve better than this!' you say to yourself. Maybe you are feeling a little sorry for yourself. 'Why does it always seem to be me that has to suffer?' you ask. But such questions are unanswerable, and you know it even as you ask them.

God would have you take your troubles to him — and leave them there! Trust him as he works in your life, that he has never made any mistakes with any of his children. Learn to rest in the knowledge that through all this pain he wants you to call upon him and discover the freshness of his grace. Let the Scriptures be the source of renewed comfort as you discover again how appropriate they are to meet your need. Learn to look at Jesus, and looking, bow in humble submission, realizing that whatever pain we have, it is nothing in comparison with what he bore for us. Learn to do as he did, 'who for the joy that was set before him endured the cross, despising the shame, and has sat down at the right hand of the throne of God' (Heb. 12:2).

Our trial is but for a moment. Soon we shall be in heaven! O Jesus, Jesus, Jesus!

Psalm 22

'My God, my God, why have you forsaken me?
Why are you so far from helping me,
And from the words of my groaning?
O my God, I cry in the daytime, but you do not hear;
And in the night season, and am not silent.

But you are holy,
Who inhabit the praises of Israel.
Our fathers trusted in you;
They trusted, and you delivered them.
They cried to you, and were delivered;
They trusted in you, and were not ashamed.

But I am a worm, and no man;
A reproach of men, and despised of the people.
All those who see me laugh me to scorn;
They shoot out the lip, they shake the head, saying,
"He trusted in the Lord, let him rescue him;
Let him deliver him, since he delights in him!"

But you are he who took me out of the womb;
You made me trust when I was on my mother's breasts.
I was cast upon you from birth.
From my mother's womb
You have been my God.
Be not far from me,
For trouble is near;
For there is none to help.

Many bulls have surrounded me;
Strong bulls of Bashan have encircled me.
They gape at me with their mouths,
As a raging and roaring lion.

I am poured out like water,
And all my bones are out of joint;
My heart is like wax;
It has melted within me.

My strength is dried up like a potsherd,
And my tongue clings to my jaws;
You have brought me to the dust of death.

For dogs have surrounded me;
The assembly of the wicked has enclosed me.
They pierced my hands and my feet;
I can count all my bones.
They look and stare at me.
They divide my garments among them,
And for my clothing they cast lots.

But you, O Lord, do not be far from me;
O my strength, hasten to help me!
Deliver me from the sword,
My precious life from the power of the dog.
Save me from the lion's mouth
And from the horns of the wild oxen!
You have answered me.

I will declare your name to my brethren;
In the midst of the congregation I will praise you.
You who fear the Lord, praise him!
All you descendants of Jacob, glorify him,
And fear him, all you offspring of Israel!
For he has not despised nor abhorred the affliction of the afflicted;
Nor has he hidden his face from him;
But when he cried to him, he heard.

My praise shall be of you in the great congregation;
I will pay my vows before those who fear him.
The poor shall eat and be satisfied;
Those who seek him will praise the Lord.
Let your heart live for ever!

All the ends of the world
Shall remember and turn to the Lord,
And all the families of the nations
Shall worship before you.
For the kingdom is the Lord's,

And he rules over the nations.
All the prosperous of the earth
Shall eat and worship;
All those who go down to the dust
Shall bow before him,
Even he who cannot keep himself alive.

A posterity shall serve him.
It will be recounted of the Lord to the next generation,
They will come and declare his righteousness to a people who
will be born,
That he has done this.'

12.
Abandoned

Psalm 22

It is impossible to over-emphasize the importance of the cross and the empty tomb for the Christian faith. For the believer, they signal the end of sin, and the certainty of glory. Just as in golf, it is vital to keep your eye on the ball, so in the Christian life, it is vital to keep your eye on the cross and the empty tomb. Christian maturity depends upon it: 'Therefore we also, since we are surrounded by so great a cloud of witnesses, let us lay aside every weight, and the sin which so easily ensnares us, and let us run with endurance the race that is set before us, looking unto Jesus, the author and finisher of our faith, who for the joy that was set before him endured the cross, despising the shame, and has sat down at the right hand of the throne of God' (Heb. 12:1-2). This is exactly what Psalm 22 is designed to do.

Nothing in David's life accounts for the events depicted in this psalm. Sometimes when David writes, he speaks, not so much about himself, but as a prophet. On the Day of Pentecost, Peter, referring to another psalm (132), finds the psalmist making a reference to the resurrection and continues: 'Therefore being a prophet ... he, foreseeing this, spoke concerning ... the Christ' (Acts 2:30-31). Psalm 22 is just like that. David was inspired by the Holy Spirit to picture the crucifixion of Jesus Christ — a thousand years before it happened!

One of its verses (v. 22) is picked up by the New Testament and seen as a reference to Christ (Heb. 2:12). As far as the New Testament is concerned, then, this psalm is a messianic psalm, one that foreshadows the coming Saviour. As we read it we are to focus our eyes upon Jesus.

The shadow of the cross falls deeply onto the pages of the Old Testament, reminding us that God was preparing his people, even then, for this crucial event. David's psalms in particular sharpen the Old Testament's focus on the coming Saviour. No psalm does this more clearly than the twenty-second, with its opening lament:

'My God, my God, why have you forsaken me?
Why are you so far from helping me,
And from the words of my groaning?'

This was to become Jesus' 'orphan cry' (or 'cry of dereliction') upon the cross.

When, after the resurrection, Jesus took the two depressed and somewhat confused disciples through the Bible on that seven-mile journey from Jerusalem to Emmaus, he must surely have opened up these words to them (Luke 24:13-35). David had his moments of anguish, it is true; but only Calvary fully explains the true significance of such a cry.

Like Psalms 3, 42, 43, 69 and 83, this psalm is what is sometimes known as a 'lament' psalm. Something is bothering the psalmist — and he is letting God know all about it. But the psalm is not all darkness. Immediately following this cry, the psalmist appeals to God's covenant as if to say, 'But you have promised!' (see vv. 3-5). It reminds us that even in the very worst of circumstances — and nothing gets worse than the feelings expressed here — we can still cling on to God's promise. The psalm teaches us most about Jesus and his death for us on the cross. But it also teaches us to persevere in tribulation and remain steadfast — even when the lights go out.

At least eight events mentioned in this psalm were fulfilled in the six hours Jesus hung on the cross, including his cry of dereliction (v. 1), the jeering of the crowds (vv. 7-8), the fact that all forsook him (v. 11), the thirst he experienced (v. 15), the crucifixion itself (v. 16), his nakedness (v. 17), the casting of lots for his garments (v. 18) and the triumphant cry, 'It is finished' (v. 31). And then there is the reference to Jesus' resurrection (vv. 27-30).

The crucifixion

According to one hymn-writer, there is much profit to be gained from meditating upon the cross:

Sweet the moments, rich in blessing
Which before the cross I spend,
Life and health, and peace possessing
From the sinner's dying Friend.

(Walter Shirley).

Another expreses a similar idea:

Near the cross! O Lamb of God,
Bring its scenes before me;
Help me walk from day to day
With its shadow o'er me.

(Fanny J. Crosby).

It is quite extraordinary how graphically the cross is portrayed in this psalm: 'They pierced my hands and my feet' (v. 16).

Crucifixion is thought to have been an invention of the Persians, who worshipped a god of the ground called Ormayed. So as not to defile the ground, executions were performed by lifting the victims into the air. Alexander the Great introduced the practice into Egypt and Carthage. The Romans are thought to have copied it from the Carthaginians.

Flavius Josephus, the famous Jewish historian and an adviser to Titus during the siege of Jerusalem, had observed many crucifixions and called them 'the most wretched deaths'. Hardened Roman soldiers often felt pity for their victims. The process was excruciatingly awful. Swelling wounds, congealing blood and raging fever combined to make crucifixion a painful ordeal. For six hours, from 9.00 to 3.00, Jesus endured it.

In Gethsemane, Jesus had shown his instinctive and understandable dread of this cruel death. He had asked for another cup to drink — if one was available; he had perspired so as to appear to bleed: 'And being in agony, he prayed more earnestly. And his sweat became like great drops of blood falling down to the ground' (Luke 22:44). But no other way was possible for the Son of God to fulfil his mission to provide an atonement for sin.

Upon reaching the place of execution, his back torn to shreds by the whipping received earlier that morning (Matt. 27:26), Jesus was nailed to the crossbar that he, and later Simon of Cyrene, had carried.

Doubt has often been expressed about the use of nails in Roman crucifixions. But in 1968, the archaeologist V. Tzaferis discovered four cave-tombs at the site of Giv'at ha-Mivtar (Rasel-Masaref) just north of Jerusalem near Mount Scopus. Amongst the discoveries were that of an ossuary inscribed with the name Yohanan Ben Ha'galgal containing the bones of an adult male and a small child. Both victims had been crucified using large seven-inch nails, and the tomb was dated as belonging to the first century A.D.[1]

We often speak of 'Calvary' rather than the more correct 'Golgotha'. Partly this is due to a misunderstanding of Luke 23:33, which tells us that 'When they had come to the place called Calvary, there they crucified him, and the criminals, one on the right hand and the other on the left.' The word Luke uses, translated in the New King James Version as 'Calvary', is the Greek word *Kranion*, meaning 'skull' (cf. our English word 'cranium'). The New International Version, on the other hand, retains the more correct reference to 'the Skull'. Luke was simply putting into Greek the Semitic word for 'skull'. Calvary refers to a certain spot, and has been used in translations from the Latin Vulgate (the Latin word for 'skull' is *calva*).

We tend to want to sanitize the cross. We sing, 'There is a green hill far away...' Golgotha, however, was more than likely a desolate place, outside the northern wall of Jerusalem, on a hill near the city wall (John 19:20), and not far from the road where passers-by could gaze and be warned (Matt. 27:39).

The cross was central in apostolic preaching: 'But God forbid that I should glory except in the cross of our Lord Jesus Christ, by whom the world has been crucified to me, and I to the world' (Gal. 6:14). All that Jesus did can be summarized this way: 'Having made peace through the blood of his cross' (Col. 1:20).

This is remarkable when we recall just how scandalous the cross was to the Jews, and how foolish it was to the Gentiles.[2] On the Day of Pentecost Peter, having blamed the event upon the Jews of Jerusalem (Acts 2:23), nevertheless saw it as being in accordance with divine purpose: 'Him, being delivered by the determined counsel and foreknowledge of God, you have taken by lawless hands, have crucified, and put to death' (Acts 2:23). God had planned it this way. Later, both Peter and Paul refer to Jesus' 'crucifixion', 'execution' and 'sufferings' (Acts 2:36; 4:10; 13:28; 17:3).

Then a curious thing emerges in Acts: both Peter and Paul refer to crucifixion as 'hanging on a tree' (Acts 5:30; 10:39; 13:29). The reason for this seems clear enough. Deuteronomy 21:22-23 gave instructions that the body of a man, who had been executed by hanging, had to be taken down before nightfall, 'for he who is hanged is accursed of God'. By calling the cross 'a tree' they were clearly identifying what happened to Jesus with Old Testament interpretations of criminal offenders. Jesus, in being crucified, was under a curse. And yet they were not ashamed or reluctant to proclaim the fact (1 Cor. 1:18-25).

There is no getting away from it: the cross is meant to signify the ugliness of sin. Think of the Old Testament sacrifices. It was altogether different from going to church on a Sunday morning! To acquire forgiveness one would have to slaughter an animal: cut its throat, drain its blood, have it disembowelled and burnt. It was nauseating — even for the most experienced worshipper. It was surely designed to show how ugly and foul a thing sin is, and how difficult to atone for. The cross of Jesus Christ does that too.

They pierced his hands and feet — those hands which had raised the dead and fed the 5,000; those feet which travelled the length and breadth of Palestine to preach the good news.

Crucifixion is a terrible thing. The crucifixion of Jesus Christ was man's greatest crime.

Dividing his garments

'They divide my garments among them, and for my clothing they cast lots' (v. 18).

Medieval and Renaissance paintings of Jesus (and modern-day films of the life of Christ) depict the crucifixion other than as it actually was. Jesus is portrayed as wearing some kind of loincloth. Perhaps we cannot, dare not, imagine it otherwise. But the possibility is that Jesus was crucified naked. Every Roman execution was done this way.[3]

Ever since the Fall man has felt ashamed of his nakedness (Gen. 3:7). Sin has made us ashamed of what we are and we hide ourselves behind clothes. For us, there is something undignified about nakedness. Think of those pictures of the Jews in Nazi pogroms being led away to gas chambers, naked, stripped of the last vestige of dignity and self-respect. The nakedness of animals is quite different. No embarrassment arises at the sight of an African elephant or a galloping horse. In fact, the sight of poodles wearing ornate garments is often laughable and out of place.

But for man it is different, because man *is* different. He is made in the image of God. No other creature on God's earth has this dignity. Man, as the climax of God's creative powers, is set apart to reflect in his being something of the nature of God himself. There is something extraordinarily special about man, that not even the Fall has entirely obliterated. The wearing of clothes is a way of expressing that we are not now what we were meant to be.

To be naked in public must be one of the greatest indignities. At the end of the twentieth century, with the advent of 'soft pornography', nakedness is no longer considered a shame. But to Christ, and those who watched the crucifixion who loved him, it must have been humiliating.

Mark tells us that the division of Jesus' garments took place 'at the third hour' (i.e. 9 o'clock in the morning, Mark 15:24-25). A condemned man was taken to the place of execution by a detachment of soldiers under the command of a centurion. Soldiers normally received the victim's clothes (shoes, head-gear, tunic, belt, outer robe). Usually, the detachment would consist of four soldiers and it is possible that four pieces were allotted between them (sandals, head-gear, belt and loincloth — the outer robe had already been taken away), leaving a fifth (the seamless inner garment) to be decided by the casting of lots.

The tunic would normally have been made of two pieces of material, sown in such a way that the seam came horizontally at waist-level. When it was purchased it was almost like a sack, the slits at the armholes having to be made after purchase as proof that the garment was new. It could be made of wool, linen, or even cotton, depending on the wealth of the purchaser. Occasionally, it was made of goat's-hair, the irritating nature of which was thought to be an aid to mortification.

Jesus' tunic was seamless. Looms large enough to accommodate the length of such a garment became available only in Jesus' own lifetime. Josephus points out that, in his day, the high priest also wore a seamless tunic.[4] Much has been made of this fact. Origen saw in it a reference to the wholeness of Jesus' teaching. Cyprian spoke of the unity of the church and Cyril managed to see in it the virgin birth.[5] Modern commentators (following John Calvin) have seen a reference to the perfect righteousness of Christ now imputed to the sinner as the basis of justification.[6]

Certainly the Bible alludes to garments as a picture of righteousness:

'I delight greatly in the Lord...
For he has clothed me with garments of salvation
And arrayed me in a robe of righteousness'

(Isa. 61:10).

Thus John Calvin's comment is a model of sobriety in understanding the 'jumble sale at the cross': 'For the evangelists exhibit the Son of God stripped of his garments, in order to inform us that by his nakedness we have obtained those riches which make us honourable in the presence of God. God determined that his own Son should be stripped of his raiment, that we, clothed with his righteousness and with the abundance of all good things, may appear with boldness in company with the angels, whereas formerly our loathsome and disgraceful aspect, in tattered garments, kept us back from approaching to heaven.'[7]

The orphan's cry

Among all the words Jesus uttered on the cross the 'cry of dereliction' is the most famous: '*Eloi, eloi, lama sabbachthani*', which is Aramaic for: 'My God, my God, why have you forsaken me?' (Mark 15:34). They are the words which open this psalm (v. 1). It is tempting to think that Jesus learnt this psalm as a boy, even then preparing himself for the cross that was before him. Never had these words become so meaningful to him as now.

Jesus had been crucified. Man's most terrible act of injustice had been perpetrated. They had crucified the Lord of glory. Three words from the cross had already been uttered, whereby he asked forgiveness for his prosecutors, showed the dying thief the way to heaven and committed his mother to the care of John. Gradually the excruciating pain of the cross enveloped him.

There was something extraordinary about this moment, more so than any other of the six hours Jesus hung on the cross. The light refused to shine. It is as though the sun itself was ashamed to behold this terrible spectacle. In the thick, heavy darkness Christ met his obligations to the few men and women who remained. Now he stands face to face with God. The ground refuses to sustain his weight; the sun denies its warmth; the mocking dies away; the sneering voices are hushed and Jesus is alone. 'Jesus ... that he might sanctify the people with his own blood, suffered outside the gate' (Heb. 13:12). He was condemned.

Calvary was the culmination of Jesus' sufferings as our substitute. Some have thought that Jesus was expressing a note of unbelief at this point. At the last moment, he had hoped that his Father would have sent a host of angels to deliver him, and because he did not, Jesus was angry with God. Others have suggested that this cry was merely an expression of how Jesus felt the loneliness that we experience. In his moment of need the promises of God were of no help to him.

Neither of these explanations does justice to the reality of the situation. As John Calvin expressed it, 'If Christ had died only a bodily death, it would have been ineffectual ... Unless his soul shared in the punishment, he would have been the Redeemer of bodies alone...' And again: 'He paid a greater and more excellent a price in suffering in his soul the terrible torments of a condemned and forsaken man.[8]

Here, in this darkness, face to face with God, he endured the agony of being forsaken. He was innocent, but he had chosen to die the death that sinners deserved, taking upon himself the punishment that sin warranted. Here the justice of God and the obedience of Christ meet. And however difficult it was for Christ to endure the physical suffering of the cross, the burden of God's unmitigated wrath was infinitely greater. Jesus the Son of God was forsaken — by God! Prayer was denied him; recourse to the assurance of his own sonship was withdrawn; whatever he had known earlier that nourished and comforted him was now taken away. Now he could not even say 'Abba'. It would appear that even the certainty of victory was clouded by the immensity of the suffering. The veil of sin was so thick that nothing could penetrate it. This is Immanuel's orphan cry.

When Luther tried to understand these words he shut himself in his room and refused to eat or answer when called. Later he was heard to cry out, 'God forsaken by God! Who can understand that?'

If we would recall the agonies of Jesus Christ for us on the cross we would surely not sin as we do. Christ endured all of this that we might be forgiven! He uttered this terrible cry that the gates of heaven might be opened up for us.

Up until this hour Jesus had not been alone: 'I am not alone, because the Father is with me' (John 16:32). But here it is different. The Father has thrust him away. It is the recoil of holiness to the presence of Jesus' imputed sin. He has to ride out this storm alone; without the awareness of his Father's upholding power he must suffer his Father's revulsion against sin.

When we think of the cross we tend only to think of the sufferings of the Son. That is understandable, of course; but Paul would have us remember that the Father, too, paid the price of love: 'For when we were still without strength, in due time Christ died for the ungodly. For scarcely for a righteous man will one die; yet perhaps for a good man someone would even dare to die. But God demonstrates his own love toward us, in that while we were still sinners, Christ died for us' (Rom. 5:6-8)

Paul says of the Father what we would expect him to say of the Son! It is the love of God, the Father, that is demonstrated on the cross! Just as Abraham felt the pain as he lifted up the knife to slay his own 'beloved' son, Isaac on Mount Moriah, so 'in the darkness of Calvary, the Father, too, paid the price of love.'[9]

It seems that even the awareness of his sonship was veiled from his consciousness at this time. He did not cry, 'My Father, my Father...,' but 'My God, my God...'

One of the Bible's words for God's response to sin is 'to vomit'. Unpleasant as the concept is, we cannot evade the graphic portrayal of God's detestation of sin: Jesus threatens to 'spit' the lukewarm Laodicean church out of his mouth (Rev. 3:16 where the Greek verb *emeo* literally means 'to vomit'; cf. Lev. 18:25-28; 20:22-23; Num. 21:5; Ps. 95:10).

The rejection of Jesus

'But I am a worm, and no man;
A reproach of men, and despised of the people.
All those who see me laugh me to scorn;
They shoot out the lip, they shake the head...'

(vv. 6-7).

The rejection of Jesus could hardly be more graphically portrayed than in these words.

Judas had betrayed him for thirty pieces of silver, fulfilling some words from another psalm: 'Even my close friend, whom I trusted, he who shared my bread, has lifted up his heel against me' (Ps. 41:9, NIV). Peter and John had fled into Jerusalem, the rest making a hasty retreat to Bethany when the soldiers came to arrest him. Peter vehemently denied any connection with Jesus of Nazareth! Three times the vacillating Pilate had tried to clear his paper-thin conscience by insisting to the crowds that he could find no fault in Christ. But they had cried, 'Crucify! Crucify!'

In particular the Gospels lay stress on the rejection of Jesus by the Jews and the priestly aristocracy. They had not only rejected him; they had also mocked him. Soldiers in the Praetorium had ridiculed him by dressing him up in a purple robe and placing a crown of thorns upon his head. They had bowed to him in pretentious worship. They even blindfolded him, prodding him to see if he could tell them which one had done it. Their contempt had been displayed as they spat in Jesus' face (Matt. 27:27-31).

Then, during the crucifixion itself, the chief priests and elders had said, 'If you are the Son of God, come down from the cross' (Matt. 27:40); and again: 'He saved others; himself he cannot save. If he is the King of Israel, let him now come down from the cross, and we will believe him' (Matt. 27:42). This is clearly foretold in Psalm 22:8: 'He trusted in the Lord, let him rescue him; let him deliver him, since he delights in him!'

Even creation rejected the Son of God as he was lifted up from the ground in total darkness.

Perhaps you imagine that had you been there you would have reacted differently. You imagine yourself standing by him in his hour of great need. But you would not! That's the awful truth of it. Not one of us would have reacted any differently to those in Jerusalem. Think of that today as you meditate upon this psalm. Think of how wretched is the sin in your heart to treat the sinless Son of God this way.

'I thirst'

'My strength is dried up like a potsherd,
And my tongue clings to my jaws;
You have brought me to the dust of death'

(v.15).

Jesus was not quoting this psalm directly when he cried, 'I thirst!' (John 19:28), but rather this is the fulfilment of Psalm 69:21. But it is quite probable that these words likening his mouth to a dried-up potsherd were on his mind too.

This was Jesus' fifth saying from the cross. Already he had asked his Father to forgive his accusers (Luke 23:34), assured a dying man that before nightfall he would be in paradise (Luke 23:43), committed his grieving mother to the care of John (John 19:26-27) and cried the orphan's lament: 'My God, my God, why have you forsaken me?' (Matt. 27:46).

Crucifixion was a terrible way to die. It spared nothing in terms of pain and consequent fever. Before the crucifixion they had offered him wine mixed with myrrh, which he had refused (Mark 15:23; Matthew says it was wine mixed with 'gall' — referring to the taste). Some have thought that this is a reference to Proverbs 31:6-7 — a custom whereby women prepared a drink of wine and frankincense as a narcotic to dull the pain. There is no mention of any women present at this point, and it is doubtful whether such a drink would have had much effect upon pain. This gesture, together with the later one whereby in response to the cry, 'I thirst', soldiers dipped a sponge in 'sour wine' (something which John tells us Jesus *did* drink, John 19:29-30) was one of cruelty and not compassion. Even a cup of cold water was denied him!

Two factors are highlighted by this cry.

1. *The true humanity of Jesus*

The incarnation was a real phenomenon. It was not a pretence. Jesus possessed a real body and soul. His body was sensitive to pain.

Sometimes when we are hurt, we tell ourselves that no one understands what we are going through. But that is not true. Jesus knows and sympathizes with us when we are hurt. He knows all about suffering (Heb. 2:14-18; 4:14-16). As the Scottish paraphrase puts it, 'In every pang that rends the heart, the Man of Sorrows has a part.'

2. *The immensity of Jesus' sufferings*

In the psalms, the expression 'I thirst' means to long for God (Ps. 42:2; 63:1). Following as it does the words, 'My God, my God why

have you forsaken me?' the expression 'I thirst' possibly had more
significance than mere physical thirst. He had passed through hell.
He had suffered what sin deserves. He had been forsaken by God.
Every ounce of his being now cried for God to return.

There is a very striking parallel here with the words that Jesus put
on the lips of the rich man in hell. In that parable, the rich man is
crying out for water to cool his tongue. Such is Jesus' picture of what
the wrath of God is like, and it is humbling to think that now he was
undergoing this torment for us.

'It is finished'

The last verse of Psalm 22 reads like this: 'They will come and
declare his righteousness to a people who will be born, that he has
done this' (v. 31). In certain manuscripts the ending of the psalm
reads like this: 'what the Lord *has done*'. It is tempting to think that
these words were also on Jesus' mind as he came to end of his
sufferings and cried, 'It is finished!' (John 19:30). In the Greek it is
just one word, *tetelestai*. It is the most encouraging word in all the
Bible! If I were asked to pick just one word from the Bible to
encourage a soul in trouble, I would choose this word. The other
Gospels explain it further: 'And when Jesus had cried out again in
a loud voice, he gave up his spirit' (Matt. 27:50). 'With a loud cry,
Jesus breathed his last' (Mark 15:37, NIV). 'Father, into your hands
I commit my spirit' (Luke 23:46, NIV; cf. Ps. 31:5).

1. Jesus is in control of his death

All through his life Jesus had seen his calling as one of obedience to
his Father's will. At his baptism in the river Jordan he had said, in
answer to John's protest, 'Permit it to be so now, for thus it is fitting
for us to fulfil all righteousness' (Matt. 3:15). Later, he became more
specific: 'But I have a baptism to be baptized with, and how
distressed I am till it is accomplished!' (Luke 12:50). 'Jesus said to
them, "My food is to do the will of him who sent me, and to finish
his work"' (John 4:34). 'For I have come down from heaven, not to
do my own will, but the will of him who sent me' (John
6:38). 'Therefore my Father loves me, because I lay down my life
that I may take it again' (John 10:17). 'No one takes it from me, but

I lay it down of myself. I have power to lay it down, and I have power to take it again. This command I have received from my Father' (John 10:18).

John Calvin perceptively saw the importance of obedience for a correct understanding of the work of Christ: 'Now someone asks, "How has Christ abolished sin, banished the separation between us and God, and acquired righteousness to render God favourable and kindly toward us?" To this we can in general reply that he has achieved this for us by the whole course of his obedience.'[10] And though the entire course of Jesus' life was a demonstration of his obedience, the climactic aspect of it is seen at Golgotha. It is here, supremely, that he finished the work of redemption.

2. This spells the end of the Old Testament

From the Garden of Eden onwards, the Old Testament had prophesied the coming of Christ (Gen. 3:15). As the Bible unfolds, more and more details concerning the coming of Christ are given: his birth (Isa.7:14), his birthplace (Micah 5:2), the flight into Egypt (Hosea 11:1) and his death (Ps. 22; Isa. 53). Every fascinating detail has now been fulfilled.

So, too, has all the Old Testament ceremonial law been accomplished. All the rites and ceremonies, depicting as they did the work of Christ, have been fulfilled in the death of Jesus. Three of the Gospels tell us that something quite extraordinary took place at this moment: 'And behold, the veil of the temple was torn in two from top to bottom' (Matt. 27:51); 'Then the veil of the temple was torn in two from top to bottom' (Mark 15:38); 'Then the sun was darkened, and the veil of the temple was torn in two' (Luke 23:45). This curtain separated the Holy Place from the Holy of Holies (e.g. Exod. 26:31-35; 27:21; 30:6; 2 Chr. 3:14). Its tearing in two signifies that the way into the presence of God (represented by the Holy of Holies in the tabernacle) has now been opened. Every barrier separating God from the sinner has been ripped apart.

It would no longer be necessary for worshippers to bring bulls and goats to an altar for sacrifice. All the ritual of blood-letting was by way of symbolizing the blood of Christ which alone can atone for sin: 'For it is not possible that the blood of bulls and goats could take away sins' (Heb. 10:4). On the other hand, 'The blood of Jesus Christ his Son cleanses us from all sin' (1 John 1:7).

3. This underlines the fact that salvation is not of works

The cry of victory assures all who place their faith in Jesus Christ of salvation and eternal security. But it equally emphasizes that salvation is by faith *alone* in Jesus Christ *alone*. As I have written elsewhere, 'Every religion apart from evangelical Christianity has the same basic flaw: each rings the changes on self-salvation. Being saved is construed as something we do; redemption is God's reward for a work well done, a payment given for services rendered. The Bible insists that it is otherwise, for as the Reformers so eloquently expressed it, salvation is by faith *alone* without any obligation to work for it; it is by grace *alone* without any sense of earning it; it is by Christ *alone* without there being any room or need for any other mediatorial agent (priest, saint, or virgin); it is by Scripture *alone*, there being no other ground of authority; and all the glory must be given to God *alone*, there being no place for self-congratulation.'[11] 'It is finished' signifies all of this.

'I will declare your name'

Reading Psalm 22 carefully reveals a definite change at verse 22. Suddenly the mood is quite different. The reason is given in verse 26:

'For he has not despised nor abhorred the affliction of the
    afflicted;
Nor has he hidden his face from him;
But when he cried to him, he heard'

(Ps. 22:24).

What follows is a 'song of praise'. The background to these words lies in the thank offering (see Lev. 7:11-18). A worshipper in deep distress would pray to God for deliverance, and make a vow to bring an offering of praise when the prayer was heard. At the fulfilment of this vow a celebration would be made, where friends, household servants and especially the Levites would be invited to join in a feast (Deut. 12:17-19). The one whose vow was being fulfilled must recall before the assembled multitude all that the Lord had done for him.

There is more to these words than David's rule would ever know. David is anticipating the deliverance and victory song of the Messiah. This is what the author of Hebrews saw when attributing these words to Christ in his exaltation: 'For it was fitting for him, for whom are all things and by whom are all things, in bringing many sons to glory, to make the author of their salvation perfect through sufferings. For both he who sanctifies and those who are being sanctified are all of one, for which reason he is not ashamed to call them brethren, saying: "I will declare your name to my brethren; in the midst of the congregation I will sing praise to you"' (Heb. 2:10-12).

How appropriate that Christ should now sing praises to his Father! The agony of crucifixion is over. The wrath of God against sin has been dealt with. Sin has been atoned for. Jesus has experienced the awful darkness and has now emerged victorious. His Father's arms are now wrapped tightly around him. The veil that surrounded him during his incarnation is now taken away. He has been glorified with the glory he had before coming into this world (John 17:1-5). His prayer has been answered.

When Christians are asked to make good their claim that Christianity is uniquely true, they point to the resurrection. Several things emerge from the phenomenon of the empty tomb. It shows at a glance that Jesus was more than a man, that his claim to being the Son of God was true. It placed a seal upon every word he uttered. It attested to the completion of his work of atonement for sin. It confirmed his present cosmic rule over the universe, foreshadowing his reappearance one day as its Judge. Moreover, the resurrection guarantees Jesus' personal pardon, presence and power in the lives of those who know him. Supremely, it depicts more clearly than anything else the fact that one day his disciples will share a similar transforming experience in the world to come. That is why he celebrates at the conclusion of this psalm.

And what a victory he celebrates! 'Posterity will serve him; future generations will be told about the Lord...' (v. 30, NIV). A psalm that has begun in the depths of despair has ended in a note of triumph and victory. The covenant of God is sure. His people will be gathered in. The church will be gathered from all the corners of the globe, and in every generation.

As we saw ealier, Psalm 22 has been described as a 'lament' psalm. This is only partly true. The ending of the psalm is one of celebration and certainty of victory. Three keywords highlight the essence of this celebration.

1. Brothers

Jesus is not ashamed to refer to his disciples as his 'brothers' (v. 22; cf. Heb. 2:12). Not only in the incarnation, but also in his exalted state, Jesus identifies himself with us. Apart from sin, he is like us in every way (Heb. 4:14-16). What an incentive that must prove to be to weary, hurt Christians who are troubled by Satan, provoked by the world, and disappointed by friends! There is not an experience that he does not share with us. However dark the way, he has gone before us and is able and willing to help us through it.

2. Praise

Four times the psalmist gives expression to praise in the closing verses (vv. 22, 23, 25, 26). It is as though we are being reminded that celebration is the pre-eminent Christian response. There is no psalm darker than this one, and yet it finds its conclusion in eulogy. That should tell us something about the way we should live our lives. If only we remembered more often than we do the fact that Jesus has risen from the dead, that even now he is at work calling out sinners into fellowship with himself! There is a purpose running through this life which is his; having seen it, all we can do is praise him.

3. King

Jesus is not only alive; he is King! His dominion stretches from shore to shore. If we only open our eyes, we can see him at work down the centuries into our present day and beyond.

The families of nations are going to bow to him (v. 27). The rich and mighty will bow their knees in worship (v. 29). It may not always seem apparent from the events taking place that this is so. That is why we need to recall the significance of those words Jesus uttered through David in this psalm. In one sense all was finished. In another everything was just beginning!

Psalm 119, part 5

'My soul clings to the dust;
Revive me according to your word'

(v. 25).

'Turn away my eyes from looking at worthless things,
And revive me in your way'

(v. 37).

'Behold, I long for your precepts;
Revive me in your righteousness'

(v. 40).

'Plead my cause and redeem me;
Revive me according to your word'

(v. 154).

'Great are your tender mercies, O Lord;
Revive me according to your judgements'

(v. 156).

'Consider how I love your precepts;
Revive me, O Lord, according to your loving-kindness'

(v. 159).

13.
Focus on revival

Psalm 119: Part 5

'It is time for you to act, O Lord, for they have regarded your law as void' (Ps. 119:126). How often have we felt like saying that! We glance at the world around and take stock of all that is happening. Evil is increasing, there seems to be little justice in the world, the church is moribund, God's children are weak and in trouble, compromise marks the church — and where is God? It is surely time for God to act!

The truth is that no matter how bad things may be, things are never too bad for God to act. This is a truth we can apply to ourselves, for no matter how bad we may feel, we are never too far away for God not to reach us.

Restoration, revival, renewal, reformation — call it what you will, the psalmist feels out of sorts and wants to get back into a relationship with God that is almost like a reconversion. At least that is how one Puritan writer describes the psalmist's longing here.[1] This is not so much a once-and-for-all 'second-blessing', a baptism of the Spirit that changes our life for good, raising us to a new and never before experienced realm of spiritual reality. The fact is that David asked for personal revival many times (witness his cries in Psalms 42, 43, 79, 80 and 85, written at different stages in his life).

Our spiritual lives are a bit like the ocean tides. There are high tides and low tides. And we need not be unduly discouraged that there are days when the reality of spiritual things seems on the wane. God promises to fill us with the Holy Spirit continually, especially in times when we need it the most. Experiencing fluctuation in this way is what the Bible seems to lead us to expect.

What is personal revival all about? Four features seem to show that in Psalm 119 the psalmist is on the road to spiritual recovery.

1. The desire for God's felt presence

Six times in this psalm the writer cries out for revival (vv. 25,37,40,154,156,159). Clearly, things are out of joint. He needs to recover from the decline into which his spiritual life has fallen. And recovery is what this psalm seems to want to tell us. The declension is passing and renewal is coming.

Whenever God draws near it is that he may talk to us: 'I have declared my ways, and you answered me' (Ps. 119:26). This intimacy of exchange between the psalmist and God had been interrupted, but this has now changed. A cloud had veiled the sunshine of God's presence, but the warm rays of the light of God are now piercing the gloom. Trials, sin, worldliness — any of these, or all in combination, can affect our communion with God. But here in this psalm is a man who is recovering: he is telling God *all* that is upon his heart. He holds nothing back. And the Lord is answering him. Here is evidence of God's presence — and the psalmist knows it! His prayer times show it!

2. A love for God's law

This shows itself both negatively and positively.

Negatively, he is willing to acknowledge sin. No recovery can ever be obtained without a willingness to confess to God our sins: 'Remove from me the way of lying...' he says (Ps. 119:29). Every now and then the Bible reminds us just how angry God is with this world. His wrath is revealed from heaven in so many ways (Rom.1:18). Revival is God turning his anger away.

So often in the psalms revival is seen like this: God has been angry and judgement seemed imminent, but now his anger has subsided. Take three psalms:

'We have become a reproach to our neighbours,
A scorn and derision to those who are around us.

How long, Lord?
Will you be angry for ever?
Will your jealousy burn like fire?
Pour out your wrath on the nations that do not know you,

And on the kingdoms that do not call on your name.
For they have devoured Jacob,
And laid waste his dwelling place.

Oh, do not remember former iniquities against us!
Let your tender mercies come speedily to meet us,
For we have been brought very low.
Help us, O God of our salvation,
For the glory of your name;
And deliver us, and provide atonement for our sins,
For your name's sake!'

(Ps.79:4-9).

'Why have you broken down her hedges,
So that all who pass by the way pluck her fruit?
The boar out of the woods uproots it,
And the wild beast of the field devours it.
Return, we beseech you, O God of hosts;
Look down from heaven and see,
And visit this vine'

(Ps.80:12-14).

'Restore us, O God of our salvation,
And cause your anger toward us to cease.
Will you be angry with us for ever?
Will you prolong your anger to all generations?
Will you not revive us again,
That your people may rejoice in you?
Show us your mercy, O Lord,
And grant us your salvation'

(Ps.85:4-7).

Sin forms callouses. It makes us less sensitive to the presence of God. God seems far away and sin encourages us to think that this situation is normal. Peter's recovery, after denying the Saviour publicly, came only after a time of confessing the depths of sin into which he had fallen. His weeping in the streets of Jerusalem on the night of Jesus' trial was the first step on the road to spiritual recovery (Matt. 26:74-75).

Alongside confession of sin there is a positive feature that discloses that the psalmist is on the way to recovery. It is his love for God's law. This has been a feature we have seen before in these studies in Psalm 119. To repeat it briefly here, at the end of our study, is only to do what the psalm itself does: repeat something often enough so that we do not fail to get the message! The psalmist longs to live for God and do what he says:

'Make me understand the way of your precepts...
I have chosen the way of truth;
Your judgements I have laid before me...
I will run in the way of your commandments,
For you shall enlarge my heart'

(Ps. 119:27,30,32).

3. The desire for a consecrated lifestyle

'Turn away my eyes from looking at worthless things, and revive me in your way' (Ps. 119:37). Like Joseph and Job (Gen. 39:8-9; Job 31:1), the psalmist, too, wants his life to be unspotted. He wants God's Word to govern every part of it.

This is not legalism. It is what every Christian should desire: a life of faithfulness to God. Attention to detail, especially in our walk with God, is what the psalmist wants more than anything else. It is not great experiences so much as great obedience that signals renewal.

4. A life of praise and joy

'I will run in the way of your commandments, for you shall enlarge my heart' (Ps. 119:32). God stirs our hearts in times of personal revival. 'Will you not revive us again, that your people may rejoice in you?' (Ps. 85:6). Psalm 16 tells us what fulness of joy is all about: 'In your presence is fulness of joy; at your right hand are pleasures for evermore' (v.11). What kind of person knows this joy? The psalm tells us that it is the one who knows God (v. 5), loves righteousness ('the path of life', v. 11) and loves the saints (v. 3).

When Nehemiah wanted the people to work for God he reminded them that joy is the source of strength (Neh. 8:12). Discouraged Christians are usually weak Christians. We are meant to know joy in our lives! Contrary to the way the Puritans are often portrayed (joyless, dour, severe, forbidding), joy was so important to them. To the question, 'What is the chief end of man?', they gave the answer: 'Man's chief end is to glorify God and *to enjoy him for ever.*' Joy has been God's plan from the start of things. We are meant to rejoice in the Lord always (Phil. 4:4). It is interesting that in that passage in Philippians (a letter that is centred around joy) Paul twice exhorts Christians to be joyful: 'Again I will say, Rejoice!' Paul knew how prone we are to lose joy in our lives.

For the psalmist, God is his 'exceeding joy' (Ps. 43:4). Trusting God makes him want to 'shout for joy' (Ps. 5:11); God's presence is 'fulness of joy' (Ps. 16:11); joy is what David lost after his adulterous relationship with Bathsheba (Ps. 51:8,12). And over 100 references in the psalms encourage us to rejoice with him.

We can ask the Lord to search our hearts right now. We can ask him to revitalize tired and weary hearts and despondent spirits. We can ask him to make us more sensitive to sin, more anxious to please him in everything, to ignite us with zeal for his work once more. If this book has brought you to see how the psalms can help you in your relationship with God, it will have succeeded in one of its aims. Now it's up to you!

References

Introduction
1. Cited by R. E. Prothero, *The Psalms in Human Life* (1914), p.334. See also John Sergeant, *The Life of Henry Martyn* (Banner of Truth, 1985), p.56: 'Large portions of it [the Bible] did he commit to memory; repeating them during his solitary walks...'
2. See his *Preface to the Psalms of David and others,* p.xxxvii.
3. *Ibid,* p.xxxviii.
4. See Tremper Longman III, *How to Read the Psalms,* (IVP,1988), p.65ff.
5. The psalms cited are: 2:7 (Heb.1:5; 5:5); 8:4-6 (Heb.2:6-8); 22:22 (Heb.2:12); 40:6-8 (Heb.10:5-7); 45:6-7 (Heb.1:8-9); 95:7-11 (Heb.3:7-11); 102:25-27 (Heb.1:10-12); 104:4 (Heb.1:7); 110:1 (1:13); 110:4 (Heb.5:6; 7:17,21); 118:6 (Heb.13:6); 135:14 (Heb.10:30).
6. See Longman, *How to read the Psalms,* pp.19-36. Longman picks out seven types, but concedes, 'A psalm may be assigned to different levels of genre from specific to general. In other words, we need to be flexible as we speak of a psalm's genre.'

Chapter 1
1. Thomas Boston, *Human Nature in its Fourfold State* (Banner of Truth, 1989), pp.151-2.

Chapter 2
1. See the helpful thoughts of Edmund Clowney on the subject of Christian meditation in his book *CM: Christian Meditation* (Craig Press,1979).
2. J. Owen, *Works* (Banner of Truth, 1965), vol. 7, p.280.
3. *Ibid.,* p.318.

Chapter 3
1. Jonathan Edwards, *Works* (Banner of Truth, 1974), vol. 1, 'A

Treatise Concerning Religious Affections', p.280.

2. John Calvin, *The Institutes of the Christian Religion*, trans. F. L. Battles, (The Westminster Press, 1975), vol. 1, p.35.

3. Charles Bridges, *Psalm 119* (Banner of Truth, 1974), p.1. Bridges' commentary on this psalm is one of the classics of evangelical literature.

4. Owen, *Works*, vol. 7, p.513.

5. Cited by Ernest Kevan in *The Grace of Law* (Baker, 1976), p.63.

6. For a useful summary, see Derek Kidner, *Psalms 73-150* (IVP, 1975), pp. 417-419.

7. F. Brown, S. R. Driver and C. A. Briggs, *Hebrew and English Lexicon of the Old Testament* (Clarendon Press: Oxford, 1975), p.203.

Chapter 4

1. The story of Hooper's death is vividly told in John Foxe's *Book of Martyrs*, and an abbreviated account can be found in J.C.Ryle, *Five English Reformers* (Banner of Truth, 1960), pp.35-70.

2. The precise point at which Hezekiah fell ill is a matter of dispute. E. J. Young thinks it may well have been earlier than the time of Sennacherib's invasion, see *The New International Commentary on the Old Testament: The Book of Isaiah* (Eerdmans, 1974), vol. 2, pp.507-8.

3. John Pollock, *George Whitefield and the Great Awakening*, (Lion, 1972), p.245. For a fuller account of the story, see also John Pollock, *John Wesley* (Hodder & Stoughton, 1989), pp. 207-213.

Chapter 5

1. Owen, *Works*, vol.6, p.208.

2. This is how J. A. Alexander translates verse 9: 'By what [means] can a youth cleanse his path, [so] as to keep [it] according to thy word?' See J. A. Alexander, *The Psalms: Translated and Explained*, (Edinburgh, 1864), p.483. See also the comments of Sinclair Ferguson in *Add to Your Faith* (Pickering and Inglis, 1980), p.76.

3. Owen, *Works*, vol. 6, p.315, as cited by Sinclair Ferguson, *John Owen on the Christian Life* (Banner of Truth, 1987), p.50.

4. Quoted by Thomas McCormick and Sharon Fish in *Meditation: A Practical Guide to a Spiritual Discipline* (IVP (USA), 1983), p.10.

5. Owen, *Works*, vol. 7, p. 276.
6. *Ibid.*, p.798.

Chapter 6
1. Others are Pss 3,7,18,34,51,52,57,59,60,63,142.
2. *Letters of Samuel Rutherford* (Banner of Truth, 1984), p.157, Letter 74.
3. See *Reflections on the Psalms* (Fontana, 1965), pp.23-33.

Chapter 7
1. The NIV has 'List my tears on your scroll...', though it acknowledges as an alternative reading: 'Put my tears in your wineskin.'
2. R. C. Sproul, *Chosen by God* (Scripture Press, 1986), p.26.
3. E. M. Bounds, *The Essentials of Prayer* (Baker, 1987), p.47.
4. See Calvin, *Institutes*, Book III, chapter xx.

Chapter 9
1. Dio Chrysostom, 11th Discourse, cited by Charles Colson, in *Against the Night: Living in the New Dark Ages* (Hodder & Stoughton, 1989), p.43.
2. *Westminster Confession*, Chapter 1, section vi.
3. C. S. Lewis, *Voyage of the Dawn Treader* (Fontana Lions, 1980), pp.97-101.

Chapter 10
1. David Clarkson, *Works*, (Banner of Truth, 1988), vol. 3, pp.193-4.
2. See the Preface to *Christian Hymns* (Evangelical Movement of Wales).

Chapter 11
1. *Letters of Samuel Rutherford*, pp.97-99, Letter to Lady Kenmure, dated 29 April 1634.
2. A.W. Pink, *Life of David,* (Zondervan, 1958), vol. 1, p.63.
3. Charles Colson, *Against the Night* (Hodder & Stoughton, 1990), p.35.
4. *Letters of Samuel Rutherford*, p. 157, Letter to Lady Culross, dated 30 December 1636.

5. Jerry Bridges, *Trusting God — even when life hurts* (Nav Press, 1988), p.173.

Chapter 12
1. See Josh McDowell, *The Resurrection — proven beyond doubt* (Scripture Press, 1988), p.54
2. cf. 1 Cor.1:23, where the apostle uses the two words *scandalon* and *môron*. It is interesting to think that the word 'moron' is used to describe someone really foolish. The world regarded Jesus that way!
3. Some have suggested that to avoid Jewish stipulations, the crucifixion of Jesus would have allowed him the use of some kind of loincloth. See Don Carson's comment in *The Expositor's Bible Commentary*, vol. 8, (Zondervan, 1984), p.576. For another interpretation, see K.Schilder, *Christ Crucified*, translated by Henry Zylstra, 'Christ Disrobed' Chapter 9: (Klock & Klock, 1978), pp.167-187. 'We want to avert our eyes,' writes Schilder, 'lest we should be cursed with the curse of Ham and his generation, but we may not. We *must* look on. He is greater than Noah...in the plundering of Christ's clothes an ancient prophecy has come to fufilment' (p.168).
4. *Antiquities of the Jews*, III, vii, 4, cited by Matthew Hendriksen, *The Gospel of John* (Banner of Truth, 1954), p.430.
5. See, Leon Morris, *The Gospel According to John* (Marshall, Morgan and Scott, 1971), p.809.
6. F. W. Krummacher, *The Suffering Saviour* (Moody Press, 1978), p.340.
7. J. Calvin, *Commentaries*, vol. XVII (Baker, 1981), p.298.
8. Calvin, *Institutes*, II, xvi, 10, 12.
9. Edmund Clowney, *The Unfolding Mystery: Discovering Christ in the Old Testament* (Nav. Press, 1988) p. 59.
10. Calvin, *Institutes*, II, xvi, 5.
11. Derek Thomas, *Serving the King* (Evangelical Press, 1989), p.16.

Chapter 13
1. Octavius Winslow, *The Inner Life: Its Nature, Relapse and Recovery* (1855), p.150.